American Deaf Culture

Acknowledgments

This anthology began its life in 1982, when I first taught a course in American Deaf Culture through the Department of American Studies at the University of New Mexico. That course, like so many other signed language and deafness-related courses at that university, was made possible by the support and vision of Tony Oliver. My hope was to give Tony a copy of this book as a partial repayment for his trust. His premature death robbed me of that opportunity but the sentiment remains. This book is dedicated to Tony Oliver.

I owe a debt of gratitude to the many students who have provided comments and suggestions on the various incarnations of this book on its way to the present collection. Most important, I want to acknowledge the invaluable assistance o Jeanne and Shane Page, who spent many long hours workinɡ on this manuscript; without their contribution and constant encouragement this volume would still be just an idea.

I want to express my sincere appreciation to each of the authors for allowing their work to appear in this collection. It is an honor and a privilege to be associated with such a distinguished group of writers. As editor, I can only hope that by bringing their work together in this anthology, new meanings and connections will emerge.

Finally, I thank my wife, Phyllis Wilcox, for sharing with me the joys and sorrows, pleasures and pains, of living in both (yet neither) Deaf and Hearing worlds. Her incredible drive—and struggle—to live the life she wants, to create the world of her dreams, has given me priceless insights into culture.

Sherman Wilcox

American Deaf Culture

An Anthology

Edited by

Sherman Wilcox

Linstok Press
Burtonsville, Maryland

Linstok Press, Inc.
4020 Blackburn Lane
Burtonsville, MD 20866

ISBN 0-932130-09-7

Contents

v

1

The Deaf Community and the Culture of Deaf People

Carol Padden

The _Dictionary of American Sign Language_, published in 1965 by William Stokoe, Carl Croneberg, and Dorothy Casterline, was unique for at least two reasons. First, it offered a new description of Sign Language based on linguistic principles. Second, it devoted a section to the description of the "social" and "cultural" characteristics of Deaf[1] people who use American Sign Language.

It was indeed unique to describe Deaf people as constituting a "cultural group." Professionals in the physical sciences and education of deaf people typically describe deaf people in terms of their pathological condition: hearing loss. There are numerous studies which list statistics about the types,

Reproduced by permission of the National Association of the Deaf from C. Baker and R. Battison (eds.), _Sign Language and the Deaf Community: Essays in Honor of William C. Stokoe_, 1980.

[1] I will use here a convention adopted by a number of researchers where the capitalized "deaf" is used when referring to cultural aspects, as in the culture of Deaf people. The lower-case "deaf," on the other hand, refers to non-cultural aspects such as the audiological condition of deafness.

ranges, and etiologies of hearing loss and how these physical deficiencies may subsequently affect the behavior of deaf people. But rarely had these professionals seriously attended to other equally important aspects of Deaf people: the fact that Deaf people form groups in which the members do not experience "deficiencies" and in which the basic needs of the individual members are met, as in any other culture of human beings.

Deaf people have long recognized that their groups are different from those of hearing people; in the "Deaf world", certain behaviors are accepted while others are discouraged. The discussion of the "linguistic community" of Deaf people in the *Dictionary of ASL* represented a break from a long tradition of "pathologizing" Deaf people. In a sense, the book brought official and public recognition of a deeper aspect of Deaf people's lives: their culture.

When I re-read the book, as I do from time to time, I am always appreciative of the many insights that I find about the structure of American Sign Language and the culture of Deaf people.

The Deaf Community

We commonly hear references to the "deaf community"[2]. The term has demographic, linguistic, political and social implications. There is a national "community" of deaf people who share certain characteristics and react to events around them as a group. In addition to a national community of deaf people, in almost every city or town in the U.S. there are smaller deaf communities. But what is a "deaf community?" More precisely, who are the members of a deaf community and what are the identifying characteristics of such a community?

---

[2] As will be explained in a later section, the "deaf community" as described here is not a cultural entity, thus, the capitalized Deaf adjective will not be used to describe it. This differs from earlier treatments of the deaf community such as those found in Markowicz & Woodward (1975), Padden & Markowicz (1976), and Baker & Padden (1978).

To answer these questions, we need first to look at a definition of community. Unfortunately, there is much disagreement among anthropologists and sociologists about what constitutes a "community".

George Hillery, a sociologist, evaluated 94 different definitions of "community" proposed by various researchers who have studied communities of people. In search of a definition, he singled out common features from the majority of the 94 definitions of local communities. Other sociologists such as Allan Edwards and Dennis Poplin have come to the same definition which Hillery proposes. Hillery's definition of "community" is as follows:

> 1. A community is a group of people who *share common goals* and cooperate in achieving these goals. Each community has its own goals. A goal may be equal employment opportunities, greater political participation, or better community services.
>
> 2. A community occupies a *particular geographic location.* The geography of a community determines the ways in which the community functions.
>
> 3. A community has some degree of *freedom to organize the social life and responsibilities of its members.* Institutions such as prisons and mental hospitals bring together groups of people in one locality, but the people have no power to make decisions about their daily lives and routines. Thus, we cannot call these types of groups "communities."

Communities may be small and closed, such as those we find in villages and tribes; but in large, industrialized societies, communities tend to be more mixed and are composed of several smaller groups of people. Consequently, while members of a community may cooperate with each other to carry out the goals of the community, there may also be conflicts and antagonism between various groups of people within the community. The conflicts are greater when any group within a community has low status or lacks power because it is a minority group. A good case is a borough of New York City that has Black, Puerto Rican, Jewish, and Protestant residents. The members of this community may unite over common concerns such as housing, but at the same time, they may conflict over other concerns that may benefit one group, but not another.

But how do we distinguish between *community* and *culture?*

A *culture* is a set of learned behaviors of a group of people who have their own language, values, rules for behavior, and traditions. A person may be born into a culture; he is brought up according to the values of the culture and his personality and behavior are shaped by his cultural values. Or, a person may grow up in one culture and later learn the language, values, and practices of a different culture and become 'enculturated' into that culture.

A *community*, on the other hand, is a general social system in which a group of people live together, share common goals, and carry out certain responsibilities to each other. For example, the culture of a community of people living in a small New England town is the same as that of the larger society in which they participate. And my example earlier of a New York borough is one where a community may be composed of a number of different cultural groups. A Puerto Rican person has the beliefs and the behaviors of his cultural group, but he lives in a larger community of people where he works and, to some degree, socializes with other people who are not Puerto Rican. Thus, a person's beliefs and actions are mainly influenced by his *culture*, but his work and many social activities are carried out within his *community*.

With this background, we cannot begin to define "deaf community." The term has been used in two restricted ways—either meaning only those persons who are audiologically deaf, or those persons who are a part of the culture of Deaf people. But it is clear that Deaf people work with and interact with other people who are not Deaf, and who share the goals of Deaf people and work with them in various social and political activities. Earlier definitions of "deaf community," such as Schein's study of the Washington, D.C. deaf community in 1968, included only those persons who are audiologically hearing impaired. I propose a definition which differs from earlier ones:

> A deaf community is a group of people who live in a particular location, share the common goals of its members, and in various ways, work toward achieving these goals. A deaf community may include persons who are not themselves Deaf, but who actively support the goals of the community and work with Deaf people to achieve them.

The definition I have proposed here fits well with the way Hillery defined "community." A community in New York City may be composed of different cultural groups; likewise, a deaf community has not only Deaf members, but also hearing and deaf people who are not culturally Deaf, and who interact on a daily basis with Deaf people and see themselves as working with Deaf people in various common concerns.

The culture of Deaf people, however, is more closed than the deaf community. Members of the Deaf culture behave as Deaf people do, use the language of Deaf people, and share the beliefs of Deaf people toward themselves and other people who are not Deaf.

I will now discuss some characteristics of the deaf community and then turn to describing certain aspects of the American Deaf culture.

Characteristics of Deaf Communities

Location. Each deaf community in the United States is uniquely affected by its location. For example, the identity of the Washington, D.C. community is undeniably influenced by the political and educational institutions in Washington, D.C. The Los Angeles deaf community is shaped by the fact that it is located in one of the largest urban areas in the United States. A great number of deaf people are employed in this area, and thus they make up a very large and powerful community.

Other deaf communities, smaller in size than the Washington, D.C. or Los Angeles communities, may be more closed, and some have less participation of non-Deaf people in their affairs.

Deaf people can move from one geographical location to another and enter into a new community with relative ease. They carry with them the knowledge of their culture to help them establish new community ties and learn the specific issues and operations of the new community. Thus, there are many different deaf communities across the United States, but there is a single American Deaf culture with members who live in different communities.

Language use. Since a deaf community is composed of people from different cultural groups, language use within the community is different from language use within the particular cultural group. As will be discussed in more detail in a later section, the language of the culture of Deaf people is American Sign Language (ASL). The use of ASL by Deaf people in community affairs is tolerated to some degree by community members. For example, some Deaf people prefer to use ASL in public speaking situations, and sign-to-voice interpreting is provided for them. At the same time, when Deaf people are involved in community activities which include hearing people who use English, they may choose to use a variety of Sign English. Language use at the community level is rather flexible, but within the cultural group, language is more restricted.

The distinction between community and culture allows us to explain how some Deaf people may accept, respect, and in community activities, even use the language of the majority group—English—but at the same time, they can prefer the language of their cultural group. Deaf people feel a strong identification with ASL since it is a part of their cultural background, but when they are involved in community activities, the use of another language allows them to interact with other persons who are not Deaf.

Goals. A community is a group of people in a certain geographical location who share common goals. What are the goals of deaf communities?

A primary goal of the national deaf community is to achieve public acceptance of deaf people as equals—equals in employment, in political representation, and in the control of institutions that involve deaf people, such as schools and service organizations. An equally important goal is the acceptance and recognition of their history and their use of signing as a means of communication. As an example, the National Association of the Deaf prints on its envelopes the message, "Hire the Deaf—They're Good Workers!" The message is a public exhortation of an important goal of the community: to convince the public that deaf workers are not a liability, and should be given equal employment opportunities. Many deaf communities have been pushing for media exposure of Sign Language in television programs and newspaper articles as a means of accomplishing another important goal: public recognition and acceptance of the use of signs to communicate.

The goals of deaf communities are derived primarily from the values of Deaf and hearing people in America. The values of a cultural group are represented in those attitudes and behaviors that the group considers most respected and important. Values can be positive: they can show what a group admires and respects. But values can also be negative: members of a cultural group may reject or be suspicious of certain attitudes and behaviors which they consider to be in conflict with their beliefs.

The Culture of American Deaf People

I will turn now to a discussion of some identifying characteristics of the American Deaf culture. My descriptions here are based first on intuition—my own understanding of how I grew up as a child of Deaf parents and how I interact with other Deaf people. I also consulted a number of books and articles written by Deaf people and have found several ideas and concerns repeated throughout these writings. I have picked out some of the more frequently occurring comments Deaf people make about themselves or their lives and have placed them in a framework of culture and cultural values. Some of the books I found helpful in explaining concerns of Deaf people are: Leo Jacobs' *A Deaf Adult Speaks Out* and W. H. Woods' *The Forgotten People*. The *Deaf American* magazine is another good source of information about issues that concern Deaf people.

Deaf people

What does it mean to be Deaf? Who are Deaf people?

Deaf people can be born into the culture, as in the case of children of Deaf parents. They begin learning the language of their parents from birth and thus acquire native competence in that language. They also learn the beliefs and behaviors of their parents' cultural group. When they enter schools, they serve as cultural and linguistic models for the larger number of deaf children who do not have Deaf parents and who become a part of the culture later in life.

Being Deaf usually means the person has some degree of hearing loss. However, the type of degree of hearing loss is not a criterion for being Deaf. Rather, the criterion is whether a person identifies with other Deaf people, and behaves as a Deaf person. Deaf people are often unaware of the details of their Deaf friends' hearing loss, and for example, may be surprised to learn that some of their friends can hear well enough to use the telephone.

But the most striking characteristic of the culture of Deaf people is their cultural values—these values shape how Deaf people behave and what they believe in.

Cultural values

What are some examples of values held by Deaf people?

Language. Certainly an all–important value of the culture is respect for one of its major identifying features: American Sign Language. Not all Deaf individuals have native competence in ASL; that is, not all Deaf individuals have learned ASL from their parents as a first language. There are many individuals who become enculturated as Deaf persons and who bring with them a knowledge of some other language, usually English. While not all Deaf people are equally competent in ASL, many of them respect and accept ASL, and more now than before, Deaf people are beginning to promote its use. For Deaf people who prefer to use ASL, the language serves as a visible means of displaying one of their unique characteristics. While use of ASL sets the Deaf person apart from the majority English–speaking culture, it also belongs to Deaf people and allows them to take advantage of their capabilities as normal language–using human beings.

Because Sign Language uses the hands, there is a "sacredness" attached to how the hands can be used to communicate. Hands are used for daily manual activities, gestures, and Sign Language, but not for other forms of communication that are *not* Sign Language. Deaf people believe firmly that hand gestures must convey some kind of visual meaning and have strongly resisted what appear to be "nonsense" use of hands—one such example is Cued Speech.

Deaf people frequently explain signs in terms of the "pictures" they depict. While some signs visually represent the object in some way—for example, the sign HOUSE outlines the shape of a typical house—other signs have a less clear pantomimic origin. The sign WHITE supposedly refers to the white ruffles on shirts that men used to wear. Whether the sign actually had that origin is not the point, but that the signer believes strongly that there must be "reason and rhyme" behind a sign.

Speaking. There is a general disassociation from speech in the Deaf culture. Some Deaf people may choose to use speech in community activities that involve non-Deaf people, such as mixed parties, parent education programs, or while representing the community in some larger public function. But on the cultural level, speaking is not considered appropriate behavior. Children who are brought up in Deaf culture are often trained to limit their mouth movement to only those movements that are part of their language. Exaggerated speaking behavior is thought of as "undignified" and sometimes can be interpreted as making fun of other Deaf people.

Before the 1960's and the advent of "total communication" and "simultaneous communication," many Deaf people preferred to sign with the mouth completely closed. This type of signing was considered "proper" and aesthetically pleasing. Now, usually only older Deaf people continue to sign this way. Although more mouth movement is permitted now, exaggerated **mouth movement** while signing is still not acceptable to Deaf people.

Mouthing and the use of speech represent things to Deaf people. Since speech has traditionally been forced on Deaf people as a substitute for their language, it has come to represent confinement and denial of the most fundamental need of Deaf people: to communicate deeply and comfortably in their own language. Deaf people often distrust speech communication for this reason. In speaking, the Deaf person feels she will always be at a disadvantage and can never become fully equal to hearing people who, from the viewpoint of the Deaf person, are always the more accurate models of speaking.

Social relations. As with any minority group, there is strong emphasis on social and family ties when family members are of the same culture or community. Carl Croneberg commented on this fact in the *Dictionary of ASL*. Deaf people consider social activities an important way of maintaining contact with other Deaf people. It has frequently been observed that Deaf people often remain in groups talking late, long after the party has ended, or after the restaurant has emptied of people. One reason is certainly that Deaf people enjoy the company of other like-minded Deaf people. They feel they gain support and trusting companionship from other Deaf people who share the same cultural beliefs and attitudes.

Additionally, in some cases, access to other culture members may be limited to parties, club meetings, or other social activities. This is often the case with Deaf people who work in a place that has no other Deaf employees. Thus, because the time that Deaf people spend together in a comfortable social atmosphere may be limited, they like to take advantage of social occasions where they are likely to meet their friends.

Stories and literature of the culture. The cultural values described in this paper are never explicitly stated; there are no books that Deaf children read to learn these values. Deaf children learn them through the process of training in which other Deaf people either reinforce or discourage their comments and actions. And these values are found among the symbols used in the literature of the culture. The play, *Sign Me Alice* by Gil

Eastman is a good example, or the poetry of Dot Miles in *Gestures: Poetry in Sign Language,* and many other unrecorded stories or games. Among the stories that Deaf people tell are the famous "success stories." A typical story may go like this: a *deaf* person grows up in an oral environment, never having met or talked with Deaf people. Later in life, the *deaf* person meets a Deaf person who brings him to parties, teaches him Sign Language and instructs him in the way of Deaf people's lives. This person becomes more and more involved, and leaves behind his past as he joins other Deaf people.

In much the same way that Americans support and propagate the "American Dream," these success stories reinforce the strong belief and pride Deaf people have in their way of life: that it is good and right to be Deaf.

Entering into the culture of Deaf people

An interesting perspective on being Deaf comes from deaf people who are going through a process of becoming Deaf and are beginning to assimilate the values of Deaf people. In a study that Harry Markowicz and I did several years ago, we described the conflicts that these people experience. For many people who grow up as part of the culture of Hearing people, they think of themselves as hearing people with a hearing loss. But when they encounter the new and different culture of Deaf people, they find that not all of their beliefs and values will be accepted. They experience a conflict between what they have always believed and what they must accept when they are with other Deaf people. Their success in becoming full members of the culture of Deaf people depends on how they are able to resolve the conflicts they experience.

An example of a conflict, a deaf person may value her speaking ability and may have always spoken when communicating with other people. But now she learns that speaking does not have the same positive value with Deaf people that it has with hearing people. Even though some Deaf people can hear some speech, and some speak well themselves, speaking is not considered usual or acceptable behavior within the cultural group. The deaf person finds that she must change the behavior that she has always considered normal, acceptable, and positive.

Another example of conflict between old and new behavior concerns how the eyes are used. In the American hearing culture, people are taught that staring is inappropriate, and many deaf people have learned to watch hearing people's faces for short periods of time, then look away quickly in order to avoid being thought as "stupid" or "making improper advances." But in ASL conversations, the listener is expected to watch the face of the signer throughout the conversation. Breaking eye contact between signer and "listener" too soon may be interpreted by Deaf people as "rude," "disinterested," or "trying to act hearing." There is a full range of rules about how to use the eyes in ASL conversations: Charlotte Baker discusses this in more detail in her 1977 article.

In learning the language of Deaf people, the deaf person needs to overcome her own cultural training in how the face is used. Facial expression among hearing people is typically quite restrained when compared with Deaf signers. However, movements of the eyes, face and head are an important part of ASL—they are used as a part of its grammar, and used to convey information necessary to control conversations between signers as well as to convey information about the emotion of the signer. Thus, the deaf person may experience a conflict between her upbringing, in which she is taught to limit the movements of her body and face, and her attempt to learn a new language in which she must "exaggerate" these behaviors.

Possibly the very first indication that another person is not a member of Deaf culture occurs during the ritual of introduction and exchanging names. Hearing people often introduce themselves by their first name only, and deaf people may do the same. However, Deaf people normally introduce themselves by their full names, and it is not unusual to also add which city or state they are from. This information is important to Deaf people because the cultural group is small, and maintaining ties with all members is a means of preserving group cohesiveness. In the same way that children long ago received names such as 'John's son' or 'Johnson', giving last names allows Deaf people to check the family background of the person being introduced and have additional information about that person. And when the deaf person is asked where he is "from," he may mistakenly give the city or state where he is currently living: a Deaf person would state where she went to school, or spent most of her childhood. It is important to Deaf people to ask for and give each other information about where they were raised and which schools—usually residential schools—they attended. This information allows Deaf people to identify themselves to other Deaf people in their cultural group.

Finally, an important behavior to learn is what to call yourself. In hearing culture, it is desirable to distinguish between degrees of hearing loss. "Hard-of-hearing" is more valued and indicates that the person is closer to being hearing and is more capable of interacting on an equal basis with other hearing people. However, "deaf" is viewed more negatively and usually carries the implication that the person is difficult to communicate with, or may not speak at all. Thus, a deaf person is more likely to be avoided if he calls himself "deaf." But, among Deaf people, the distinctions between hearing loss are not considered important for group relations. "Deaf" is not a label of deafness as much as a label of identity with other Deaf people. A person learning to interact with other Deaf people will quickly learn that there is one name for all members of the cultural group, regardless of the degree of hearing loss: Deaf. In fact, the sign DEAF can be used in an ASL sentence to mean "my friends," which conveys the cultural meaning of "Deaf." Although Deaf people recognize and accept members that are audiologically hard-of-hearing, calling oneself "hard-of-hearing" rather than by the group name is interpreted by some Deaf people as "putting on airs," because it appears to draw undue attention to hearing loss.

The existence of conflict brings out those aspects of the culture of Deaf people that are unique and separate from other cultural groups. It also shows that the group of Deaf people is not merely a group of like-minded people, as with a bridge club, but a group of people who share a code of behaviors and values that are learned and passed on from one generation of Deaf people to the next. Entering into Deaf culture and becoming Deaf means learning all the appropriate ways to behave like a Deaf person.

Hearing children of Deaf parents

As mentioned earlier, being Deaf usually means the person has a hearing loss. But there are hearing children of Deaf parents who have grown up with their parents' culture and feel a strong personal affiliation with other Deaf people. They are like other Deaf people in that they actively participate in various cultural affairs and consider themselves a part of the cultural group. However, the fact that they have an "extra sense," like the "sighted man in a country of the blind," is often a source of conflict for these hearing children of Deaf parents.

They may find themselves cast in the demanding role of being "links" between their families and the majority culture. At a very young age, they may learn to interpret for their families and make contact with other hearing people on behalf of the family. Even after they have left the family, they may still maintain the role of a "go-between," perhaps as professional interpreters, or as part of a Deaf organization that makes contact with hearing people.

Hearing children of Deaf parents are usually given greater access to the culture of Deaf people than other hearing children who do not have Deaf parents. Since they often have been brought up to share the cherished values of Deaf people, Deaf people perceive them as less likely to threaten or try to change the structure of the cultural group, and thus, will allow them to interact more fully with Deaf people. An equally important factor in their being able to become members of the cultural group is their knowledge of the group's language. Hearing children of Deaf parents may acquire native competence in ASL to the point where Deaf people will say, "he signs like Deaf people."

Some hearing children of Deaf parents are acutely aware that the behaviors they must use when they interact with a group of Deaf people are different from the behaviors they must use with a group of hearing people. When they are with Deaf people, they find that they must change many aspects of their behavior; the language they use, the kind of jokes they tell, or how they use their eyes. On the other hand, there are other hearing children of Deaf parents who do not seem to be as aware of conflicts between hearing and Deaf cultures. These children say that when interacting with Deaf people, they behave a certain way, but when with hearing people, they find that they switch behaviors unconsciously.

We need to study more deeply and carefully the experiences of hearing children of Deaf parents. Their varied experiences raise many questions about the characteristics of the culture of Deaf people. For one thing, their experiences will help us understand the role hearing loss plays in shaping the culture of Deaf people.

Summary

The term "deaf community" is used in many different ways. The fact that the word "community" has had different definitions has probably contributed to the variety of definitions that have been used for "deaf community." I follow the definition of community proposed by Hillery, and the term "deaf community" is used here in a more general sense than has been used before: to describe the group of people who interact and contribute to the goals of the community. These people can be members of different cultural groups, and are joined together to the extent that they share in the goals of the community as a whole.

While there is general consensus on the goals of the community, there may also be conflicts over various issues that arise in the community, resulting from the different values of each cultural group.

The culture of Deaf people has not yet been studied in much depth. One reason is that, until recently, it was rare to describe Deaf people as having a *culture*, although it has often been remarked that deaf people tend to seek out other deaf people for companionship. Descriptions of Deaf people have often focused on details of their deficiency, and not on the normal aspects of their lives: that they, like other human beings, are members of communities and cultural groups.

Values of Deaf people reflect the beliefs and ways in which Deaf people react to their social environment. These values are often different from those of the majority culture and need to be learned by incoming deaf people; this is reflected in the problems experienced by deaf people who first grow up as hearing people.

William Stokoe's perspective on the language and culture of Deaf people shows his attempt to describe Deaf people not as abnormal, pathological cases, but as individuals who have a cultural and linguistic identity. His work hopefully has begun an age in which facts about Deaf people are not hidden or ignored, but are brought out to help us reach a new stage of awareness and acceptance of Deaf people. It is only then that Deaf people can achieve the kind of equality they have long sought.

2

A Night of Living Terror

Ben Bahan

IT WAS Halloween Night at about 8:30. My doorbell flashed for what seemed to be the hundredth time. I groaned and thought, "What idiot would send their kids out this late?" Grabbing a bowl of candies, I went to the door wondering what costume this kid would be wearing; so far the scariest one was a kid with a Ronald Reagan mask. As I opened the door and glanced down at the kid, I couldn't believe my eyes. I screamed, dropped the bowl, and ran back into the house bolting the door shut behind me. The kid was dressed like a hearing person.

I woke up fast, sweating and breathing hard. I ran to my roommate, who happens to be a therapist, and turned on the light in his room. Waking from a deep sleep, he sat up in bed. I sat by him and told him about my nightmare. He interpreted my dream as an anxiety attack and told me that it would go away soon.

Little did he know that my nightmare was only the beginning of a chain of horrors. I don't intend to compete with Stephen King, horror master of our time. But remember this as you read my strange tale. King writes about horrors that exist only in his grotesque imagination. My horror stories are

Reproduced by permission of the author and *Deaf Community News*.

straight from the living realms of your, yes, YOUR reality! I may be dreaming, but my dreams are projecting truth.

Two o'clock in the morning I woke up again and ran to my roommate's room. He was becoming slightly irritated and asked, "What did you dream about this time?"

"My girlfriend went to Gallaudet college and returned a different person. I didn't know her, I couldn't even understand her!"

"Calm down. Tell me what did she do that you didn't understand?" asked my roommate soothingly.

"I didn't understand her signing. She signed sooo strange—using signs like ING, WAS, THE ..."

"Your dreams show that you have fear of difference, a fear of change. Just relax and remember its only a dream," he comforted me. I found his comfort irritating. Her signing in my dream had been so weird, so mechanical that it looked like she had undergone "robot-ization". Then I remembered—it was S.E.E., the "radiation-like contamination" of ASL.

3:00 AM: I woke again and staggered to my roommate's room, flicking on the light to tell him the details of my latest dream.

"I dreamed I was in a mainstreamed classroom, with an interpreter who was interpreting after only taking three sign language classes. I raised my hand and asked the teacher in ASL, 'YOU MEAN THAT POE WROTE HORROR STORIES?' The interpreter squinted, wet her lips and stuttered, in what was supposed to be English, 'You fork impossible Poo wrote terrible sentences.' The class roared in laughter, and the teacher looked at me as if I was some kind of idiot."

My roommate, still groggy, glanced at his clock. Realizing it was three o'clock in the morning, he screamed, "WHAT!"

"That's exactly how I feel," I replied.

It was four o'clock in the morning, when I stumbled into his room once more. I shook him, then asked, "When will Gallaudet College have a deaf president?"

"You woke me up at four o'clock in the morning to ask me that?" said my favorite therapist, obviously annoyed.

"I dreamed that I went to Gallaudet College for my 65th class reunion. At the old age of 87 I walked on campus, and was greeted by a new president, who was hearing and didn't know sign language. He was appointed over three other deaf candidates. He was the ninth hearing president appointed since my graduation. On campus a group of deaf professors were meeting. They called themselves DRCC (Deaf Related Concerns Committee). It bothered me that a college for the Deaf had to have such a group to be the watchdog of the college, making sure their culture was not being eradicated. Does Howard University need a black related concerns committee? Gallaudet is becoming the South Africa of the Deaf world!"

I was becoming hysterical.

"Calm down, calm down, before I beat the #%@*^* daylights out of you," my roommate ordered, obviously out of his therapist role. "It's only a dream. What did you drink before going to bed? Did you drink milk?"

"If I needed a nutritionist, I would have gone to my other roommate!" I replied and stormed out.

My clock read 5:03 AM. I woke up horrified, running my hands all over my face trying to feel some impairment. Not feeling anything I got up and rushed into my "therapist's" room frenetically. I flicked on the light and shook his bed hard. He got up so fast that his eyes were still closed. After waking him up, I asked, "How's my face, is it deformed?"

"What has gotten into you this time?" he asked without replying to my question.

"Is there anything wrong with my face?" I persisted.

"No, what is it?" he asked, hoping I'd go away.

"Whew. I had a terrible nightmare... the worse one yet."

"What now?" he demanded.

"I dreamed that I had agreed to undergo an experiment with a company that produces cochlear implants. I don't know how or why I agreed to do that, but I did. I went to a hospital to have the equipment surgically implanted into my mental system. While I was sedated, they cut me open and threw in the wires and machinery, and hooked it up. When I woke up, the doctors and nurses were standing by, waiting to apologize for the mishap that occurred while hooking me up. The doctor explained that the device was hooked up perfectly and should be operable once I have the outside device attached, but he explained that his assistant had made a mistake and cut a little too deep, thus cutting my facial nerve, and leaving one side of my face sagged."

"Your face seems OK to me. I think your dream implies that you have some degree of denial of your deafness but your desire to become hearing is overcome by your fear of change," my roommate consoled me sarcastically.

"What? Me deny my deafness? The heck I am: I'm too proud to undergo such cosmetic surgery!"

"It's only one possible interpretation of your dream," he stated. Nevertheless I felt insulted and returned to bed.

I woke up and felt the blood drain completely from my face. In sheer terror, I glanced around the room, watching and waiting for hints that this last dream had become reality. I realized it was too early to tell, since the sun had not yet crept over the horizon. I shuffled to my roommate's room and tapped his shoulder lightly. He jumped out of bed in deep fright, and flicked on the light. He glanced up at me looking horrified and said, "You are as pale as a ghost. What happened?"

I didn't reply. I just stood there in complete daze.

"Sit down." My roommate guided me to a seated position and asked again, "What's wrong?"

I signed, one sign at a time, very slowly, "Me Hearing."
AAAIIIIIIGGGGGHHHHHH!

3

Inside the Deaf Community

Barbara Kannapell

WHEN I think of communication the first thing that comes to my mind is the free flow of communication in the Deaf Community.[1] Deaf people feel so comfortable in communicating with each other at deaf clubs, church services for the deaf, or any event for deaf people given by deaf people, as opposed to the discomfort that they feel outside of the Deaf Community.

Then, what is communication? Eileen Paul wrote an article, "Some Notes On Communication...," in which she defines the meaning of communication which is most relevant to that in the Deaf Community:

> Usually when we try to discuss what communication is, people think it is about transmitting ideas from one person to another. In order to understand communication, we have to go deeper than that. "Communication" comes from two Latin words—"com" with an "un"—which means "one." Literally, the words mean something about "becoming one with," and it related to the word "communion." So, communication is not just a question of transmitting ideas; it is a process of sharing our feelings too.

Reproduced by permission of National Association of the Deaf from *Deaf American*, 34(4), 1982.

[1] See Carol Padden's article (this volume) for the definition of Deaf Community.

It is a process of letting another person know what things meant to us.

Communication is a process of sharing what things mean to us with ourselves and with other persons.

This last statement is the theme throughout this paper. I will show how it is relevant to the communication in the Deaf Community.

Now, let's look inside the Deaf Community. The question I'd like to ask is: "What makes deaf people feel at ease in communicating with each other?" I will offer three explanations.

The First Explanation

Deaf people can understand each other 100 percent of the time, whereas outside of the Deaf Community they get *fragmentary information* or *one-way communication*. Fragmentary information means that the deaf person may get 50, 60, or 70 percent of the information communicated through a not-so-skilled interpreter, or through a hearing person who uses speech or who has just learned Sign Language.

One-way communication can mean an interpreter who can express from voice to sign, but can't interpret from sign to voice. It can also mean a hearing person who can express him/herself in Sign Language, but cannot read the signs of a deaf person. Deaf people experience this kind of one-way communication very often when they are with hearing people.

The Second Explanation

Deaf people share a common language—American Sign Language (ASL). ASL seems to be the primary communication mode we use among ourselves. Everything else—English in different forms—is the secondary communication mode for some deaf people. It does not necessarily mean that all deaf people are fluent in ASL. It can mean that those who are not fluent in ASL are skilled in English, or it can mean that they have no skills in English. It is possible that there are deaf people who are bilingual in varying degrees. I'd like to show some variations in communication styles in the Deaf Community:

> *ASL monolinguals.* Deaf people who are comfortable expressing themselves only in ASL, and in understanding only ASL. They have no skills in English.
>
> *ASL dominant bilinguals.* Deaf people who are more comfortable expressing themselves in ASL than English, and are able to understand ASL better than English (either printed or signed English).
>
> *Balanced bilinguals.* Deaf people who are comfortable expressing themselves in both ASL and English, and who are able to understand both equally well.
>
> *English dominant bilinguals.* Deaf people who are more comfortable expressing themselves in English, and who are able to understand English (in printed English or signed English) better than ASL.
>
> *English monolinguals.* Deaf people who are comfortable expressing themselves only in English (oral or signed English) and in understanding English (in printed or oral or signed English). They have no skills in ASL.
>
> *Semi-linguals.* Deaf people who do have some skills in both English and ASL, but are not able to master either language fully.

Based on these variations, I would like to raise several questions: 1) Who is really in the core of the Deaf Community, and who is on the fringe of the Deaf Community? 2) Are English-dominant bilinguals and English monolinguals in the core of the Deaf Community, or are they on the fringe? 3) Are there deaf people who use only ASL and understand only ASL (ASL monolinguals)? In other words, are there deaf people who know absolutely no English?

Within the Deaf Community, deaf people have a complex system of evaluating who should be in the core or on the fringe of the Deaf Community. It is important to mention here that the degree of hearing loss is not the most important requirement for being in the core of the Deaf Community. Deaf people just identify themselves as deaf or hard of hearing, no matter what their degree of loss is. They do not need to show their audiogram to enter the Deaf Community. Sharing a common language seems, however, not to be enough to be admitted to the Deaf Community.

The Third Explanation

"Communication is the process of sharing what things mean to us with ourselves and with other people." I think this is the most important explanation of all. Deaf people share what things mean to each other, i.e., the word "deaf" means different thing to deaf and to hearing people. Also, the word "hearing" has a different meaning for deaf people. Deaf people communicate those meanings through ASL. Such meanings extend to the following:

The bond of communication and strong relationships. Deaf people experience a strong bond of communication because they have common topics to share which are based on common experiences, such as the history of deaf people, school experiences, family experiences, sports, movies, stories and jokes. They develop strong relations based on these common experiences with other deaf people. Many deaf people develop strong relationships during school years and maintain these relationships throughout their lives. This feeling may be carried over from residential schools, where they developed a strong bond of communication for the purpose of survival skills.

Cultural beliefs and values. Carol Padden offers a good explanation of cultural beliefs and values in her essay in this volume (Chapter One). These beliefs and values are also related to the complex system of evaluating who should be in the core of the Deaf Community and who should be on the fringe. For example, deaf people have a way of evaluating who behaves like a deaf person and who behaves like a hearing person.

If a deaf person behaves like a hearing person, other deaf people will sign "hearing" on the forehead to show "he thinks like a hearing person." Thus, he is on the fringe of the Deaf Community, depending on his/her attitudes. Conversely, if a deaf person behaves like a deaf person, other deaf people may sign "strong deaf" or "fluent ASL," which means that the person is culturally deaf. Thus, he or she is admitted to the core of the Deaf Community.

If a hearing person wants to meet a deaf person, the rules of the Deaf Community dictate that he/she must be introduced as a "hearing" person in the Deaf Community. Then, the deaf person being introduced will ask questions such as "you from Gallaudet?" or "from deaf family?" or "teach deaf children?" If the hearing person has something to do with working with deaf people, or comes from a deaf family, a deaf person would be satisfied, since this would meet his/her expectations of a hearing person. But, if the hearing person is just interested in learning ASL as a foreign language and has nothing to do with deafness, deaf people will become suspicious and on guard. It is true that a few hearing people who have nothing to do with the education of deaf children or who come from a deaf family may eventually be admitted to this Community. These are just two examples relating to cultural beliefs and values in the deaf Community.

Feeling equal. The bond of communication and strong relationships and similar cultural beliefs and values are equated with feelings of equality among deaf people. Within the Deaf Community is the only place that deaf people experience equality with others. Usually, deaf people do not feel equal with hearing people outside of the Deaf Community.

Thus, ASL is a powerful tool for identity in the Deaf Community, along with the cultural beliefs and values that are expressed through ASL. This suggests that ASL is the cultural language of the Deaf Community.

However, I want to emphasize that the knowledge of ASL alone seems not to be enough to qualify a person to be in the core of the Deaf Community. Everything else—shared common experiences, and cultural beliefs and values which are attached to ASL—also seem to be important requirements for admittance to the core of the Deaf Community. A deaf person who is in the core of the Deaf Community is considered to be "culturally deaf."

The more culturally deaf a person becomes, the further he or she moves into the core of the Deaf Community. I suggest that the Deaf Community can be compared to the majority community of hearing people in terms of language supremacy. Deaf people experience ASL supremacy in the Deaf Community similar to hearing people's English supremacy in the majority community.

In relation to deaf people's experience of ASL supremacy, we also need to look into the functions of ASL in the Deaf Community. Language can serve many functions, i.e., Pidgin Sign English functions as a way for deaf people to communicate with hearing people. ASL serves as a way for deaf people to communicate with each other, but there is much more to it than just a function of language. There is a symbolic function in relation to identity and power, and we often keep our use of ASL limited to ourselves to preserve these factors of identity and power.

As a protection of our own identities, deaf people keep thinking that hearing people cannot learn ASL, but really deaf people exert their power in using ASL. For example, we can talk about anything we want—right in the middle of a crowd of hearing people. They are not supposed to understand us. In a classroom, for example, deaf students often talk about the hearing teacher right in front of him or her. They may say "understand zero" or "it went over my head" in ASL. The hearing teacher is not supposed to understand ASL.

If hearing people understand ASL, then deaf people are no longer in power using ASL. Here is what happened to me several years ago: I realized that a deaf friend of mine and I were no longer in power using ASL in front of two hearing friends. One of them knew no Sign Language, but the other one knew ASL fairly well. As my deaf friend and I began a deep personal discussion, the hearing person who knew ASL was able to understand us and felt awkward interpreting to the other hearing person what we were talking about.

I did not expect her to understand our discussion in ASL or to interpret to the hearing person because hearing people are not supposed to understand the conversation of deaf people in ASL. That's how deaf people experience ASL supremacy. ASL is the only creation which grows out of the Deaf Community. It is our language in every sense of the word. We create it, we keep it alive, and it keeps us and our traditions alive.

I suggest another reason why deaf people do not use ASL with hearing people: Language choice reflects identity choice. Somehow, deaf people learn not to use ASL with hearing people in their school years. Deaf persons choose ASL or English depending on the identity the system wants for them. When they are with hearing people, they try to communicate in English—trying to use voice or sign in English or both at the same time. When they are with other deaf people, they feel more like themselves and use ASL, and experience a strong sense of group identity.

I also suggest that in relation to the theme of this paper again, these words, "hearing person," "speech," and "English," are equivalent. When a deaf person meets a hearing person, the word "English" is strongly attached to that hearing person, so a deaf person tries to communicate on a hearing person's terms—using voice or signing in English order or both.

All those explanations of why deaf people do not share ASL with hearing people support this statement:

"Communication is a process of sharing what things mean to us with ourselves and with other persons." This statement can be rephrased as follows: Deaf people share what things mean to them with themselves and with other deaf people. They do not usually share their own special meanings with hearing people probably because 1) Hearing people will never understand what it is like to be deaf; 2) Deaf people do not have a chance to share what things mean to them with hearing people; and/or 3) Deaf people think hearing people are not interested in hearing what we would like to share with them.

I can tell you from my experiences of sharing what the deaf experience or world means to me with deaf and hearing people. I needed to develop trust in myself before I could share my world with deaf and hearing people. The more I share with them, the more they share with me. In other words, we need to respect ourselves as deaf persons and respect our language first before we can share what the deaf world means to us with other deaf and hearing people.

In conclusion, I see this paper as only a beginning in the understanding of the meaning of communication in the Deaf Community.

4

Notes from a 'Seeing Person'

Ben Bahan

I WALKED into a dentist office and was asked by a pretty receptionist if she could help me.

"I am deaf," I said, which is the usual thing I would say to prevent any misunderstanding.

"Hi, Dave, I am Susan. Is there anything I can do for you?"

I suddenly realized she didn't understand me, so I pointed to my ear and shook my head "no."

Susan's face turned pale. I was tempted to say, "BOO," but was afraid she would have a heart attack. I could see the newspaper headlines: DEATH MAN SCARED RECEPTIONIST TO DEAF.

Hearing People Panic

Too many people freeze when they see or hear the word "deaf" when it is tagged with a person in front of them. They probably never met a deaf person before or never dreamt they'd meet one. They do not know what to do.

I have a burning desire to know what made them not know what to do. One apparent reason would seem to be: they

---

Reproduced by permission of the author and *Deaf Community News*.

aren't educated about deafness. However, they still may not know what to do even if they have some information on deafness.

I feel educating the hearing about deafness only makes the situation worse on ourselves because of the word we are labeled: deaf.

Proud to be Deaf, but...

Now I am not trying to deny my deafness. I am proud to be deaf! So proud that I feel there is a need to erase the pathological (disease) viewpoint of deafness.

Many deaf people do not feel handicapped/disabled. How do we know we are missing something if we never had it in the first place?

For example, if you grew up in a place where they served Coca-Cola at all meals, then moved to another place where they never served it, you would miss Coca-Cola.

Many deaf people do not miss hearing because they never heard in the first place. The feeling of being handicapped isn't there.

It is the hearing world that tells us we are handicapped and disabled.

The Power of Words

One powerful tool the hearing world uses to keep us handicapped is the use of the word deaf. It may seem like an irony but that is the way of Word Power. I looked in two dictionaries to see the meaning of the word deaf.

Webster's dictionary: deaf: ('def) adj. 1: lacking or deficient in sense of hearing 2: unwilling to hear or listen.

Random House dictionary: deaf: ('def) adj. 1: partially or wholly unable to hear. 2: refusing to listen.

Apparently there are two definitions. One is the inability to hear, and the other is the refusal to hear. Both definitions seem to offer negative shadowing. I will be fair and pull out the real definition that explains who I am: I am deaf—I am unable to hear.

Deaf people for years have fought to eliminate the second word that has been tagged naggingly to the word deaf: dumb and mute. We have seen a lot of results in the public's response by not using the words dumb and mute.

We have fought for our place in this society using the term deaf pride. Our language and cultural identity makes us improve the dressing of the word deaf by capitalizing the "d" as in Deaf. I might go back to the same receptionist and say, "I am Deaf with a capital 'D'."

That helps when I write it down. I feel bigger than life by capitalizing my "D". But, it still doesn't change the meaning of the word in Webster's dictionary and Random House. The receptionist would still freeze and not know what to do.

Two Suggestions

I suggest we do something about it. Either we 1) work hard trying to add another meaning to the word deaf in the dictionaries worldwide by saying Deaf can also mean a subcultural group of people who by some degree of hearing loss choose to sign and use visual means of communications; or 2) set up a new label for ourselves that is not pathological or negative.

Let us look at some minority group as an example: The blacks have made some social changes in the word describing their race. From negro to black. Although the root of the word negro goes back to Latin meaning black, historically the word has changed over time and became derogatory in general viewpoint. Today, it is not appropriate to use the word negroes.

Another group would be the gays. The term homosexual is pathological and has negative shadowings, so the use of the word gay changes the light on them.

The word deaf, when used either with or without a capital, focuses on what we are unable to do: hear. Like I have said before, many of us have never heard before and do not miss hearing because we never had it to begin with, so it is strange to put a focus on our inability to hear when we identify ourselves with other people.

This kind of identity puts us down and we are helping the world put ourselves down by using the word as it is defined in the dictionaries.

A 'Seeing' Person

I have no alternative suggestion for a better word to describe ourselves. The closest I can come is, seeing person. By using that word I put myself in a position of things I can do, instead of what I can't do. That moves the focal point off my inability and focuses on my ability.

Since I identified myself as a seeing person, that would explain everything around me: like TTYs, decoders, flashing door-bells, lipreading, and the emergence of a seeing language, American Sign Language. Come to think of it, ASL did not emerge because of what we cannot do, it emerged because of what we can do: see.

Now, the question remains: suppose the general public is now aware of the declaration of our identity as "seeing people" instead of deaf people? Suppose I returned to the receptionist and said, "I am a seeing person." Would she grab a paper immediately, or try to speak clearly knowing what we can do instead of knowing what we can't do?

What Do You Think?

The term "seeing" is just a suggestion, not a final choice. I would be more than happy hearing what you have in mind. For now, I am still proud to be deaf. At the same time, we should realize the power of words and their effects on our lives.

5

How Do You Dance Without Music?

Shanny Mow

MY NAME is Sam. Sometimes I'm called Silent Sam, a tag I loathe out of prejudice—both mine and the bestower's. Besides, it is misleading since I make more noise sipping my soup than the guy at the next table, who is not deaf, but wishes he were every time I take a particularly enthusiastic spoonful.

This is my story, of how I live through a day and the problems I face as a deaf human being, as told to and written by another deaf human being who is fortunate to have the words I do not.

I would be presumptuous to claim that my problems are typical of all deaf persons. Or that I qualify as a Typical Deaf Person, whatever that is. There are the prelingually and postlingually deaf individuals. There are the college-educated and the illiterate. And those in-between. The hard of hearing. The mentally retarded. The brain damaged. The victims of cerebral palsy. And others. You may say each is a breed apart. Each has problems of his own.

In a style that belies my blue-collar job, my recorder has set down what I think, what I believe, and what I have gone through.

Reproduced by permission of the New Mexico School for the Deaf from *Answers*, 1970.

I can dance better than I can write. Seeing me on the dance floor, hearing people always ask: How do you dance without music? Actually I don't, but I get what they mean. Vibrations, I would tell them. Then one night I realized I have been giving an incomplete answer. Now I tell them: Vibrations of life.

"But you can't see a thing from the driver's side," the Volkswagen dealer explains. Sam reads the hurried scribbling and for a minute fingers his new driver's license. Under RESTRICTIONS, it reads LEFT AND RIGHT REAR VIEW MIRRORS.

Ten dollars goodbye for a right rear view mirror that doesn't give you the view you don't need. Since when did the bureaucrats at the Motor Vehicles decide deafness is a luxury? Be grateful that they let you drive at all?

Wearily, he takes the pad and writes, "Install it anyway. I'll be back."

In the noon sun he squints but still can make out the drug store two blocks away. Carefully he looks left, then right and left again and crosses the street. Midway he pauses to look right again.

A lot can happen in two blocks. A lost motorist yelling for directions. A nervous smoker asking for a match. A friendly stranger with sinister motives wanting to talk. A policeman blowing his whistle and suspecting you for a fugitive when you walk on. A dog biting from behind. A runaway Safeway cart hitting from the blind side. You grow weary and wary of such people who, at the sight of you pointing to your ear, always seem to forget suddenly their purpose for approaching you. As for whistle-blowing policemen, biting dogs and runaway carts, you develop your own brand of oriental fatalism.

Inside the drug store Sam asks for a package of Salem Cigarettes, pronouncing the brand name as distinctly as he can. The clerk gives him an odd look, then reaches down the counter. Her hand reappears with the Salems. He breathes easier.

You feel like a poker player who is also a compulsive bluffer. Mervin Garretson has explained why he switched brands, rather than fight. As long as you pronounce something safe like Salem, not Chesterfield, there is little danger of receiving cough syrup instead. You can never relax when you cannot hear what you speak. Not even if you've been up to your ears in speech training. Maybe you can, in front of a trained ear, someone who is familiar with the "deaf accent," but unfortunately is not always around.

Sam also selects a Chapstick and a roll of Lifesavers. The clerk says something which he can at best only guess. His pocket feels heavy with change, but he reaches for his wallet, takes out a dollar bill and hands it to her.

The tension is even worse when you attempt to lipread. The name of this game is "Figure out the Fingerprint." Like the whorls on his fingertips, each person's lips are different and moved in a peculiar way of their own. When young, you build confidence as you guess correctly "ball," "fish," "top," and "shoe" on your teacher's lips. This confidence doesn't last. As soon as you discover there are more than four words in the dictionary, it evaporates. Seventy percent of the words when appearing on the lips are no more than blurs. Lipreading is a precarious and cruel art which rewards a few who have mastered it and tortures the many who have tried and failed.

The lunch hour is almost over. Sam drives back to the plant, ignoring the new chrome outside his Volkswagen. Several workers nod or wave at him as he makes his way to his workbench. He waves back, but today he feels no desire to join them for the usual noisy banter that precedes the job at hand.

These are good guys. We get along. They like you, even respect you. You laugh at their jokes and fake punches to their jaws. Yet there remains an invisible, insurmountable wall between us. No man can become completely a part of another man's world. He is never more eloquently reminded of this impossibility than when there is no way he can talk with the other man.

Without a word, the foreman nods. Sam scribbles down another question. The foreman nods again. Still another question. More nodding, this time with marked annoyance. Sam then knows it is pointless to continue.

Communication is the father of human relationships. From infancy a person learns to speak at a rate closely synchronized with his thinking processes. Deviation from this timing between thinking and speaking upsets his natural flow of thought. He loses his tongue or forces out words which sound so artificial that they disgust him. As a deaf person, you sympathize with this mental block in the hearing person who tries to speak to you. In fact, you expect it. For this reason, just or not, you always wonder why he takes the trouble to speak to you.

You feel no less helpless in your search for meaningful communication. When the hearing person does not know, as he usually does not, the sign language, the only recourse lies with the pencil and pad. Here your language defeats you before you begin. You have been deprived of the natural process of learning language, i.e. by the ear. You do not start from scratch when you begin your formal education. The itch is not even there. English is a language so complicated and inconsistent that its mastery is for you as elusive as the pot of gold at the end of the rainbow. Gamely you pick up the pencil only to find the hearing person hung-up in his own way: poor penmanship, bad spelling, or some other reasons known only to him. Inhibition reduces communication to a superficial level, a most unsatisfactory relationship to both parties. Speech and lipreading? Try discussing Kazantzakis, or any subject, limiting yourself to the thirty percent of the words that can be lipread with no guarantee that there would be none of the words you have not seen before.

Tired as he is, Sam cannot go home yet. He remembers he has a couple of errands to perform. He surveys the traffic. It is getting bad. He tries, but cannot think of a short cut to the other side of town where Paul lives. He shifts the gears, passing one roadside booth after another, each displaying the familiar Bell symbol.

His finger is tiring. From pressing continuously the door button that is rigged to a light bulb inside. He searches through a window, then another. No sign of life except for the parakeet. Refraining from kicking the door, he hastily writes down the message, inserts it in a crack in the door and returns to his car. Sweat streaks down his forehead and he wipes it away. Hopefully he eyes the door once more.

How soon will you get Paul's reply? Will the note still be there when he comes home? When will he come home? He could not know you were driving down. You took your chance and lost. An alternate to this eternal courtship with chance is to plan ahead. Carry out, no wavering. Build a reputation of a man of his word. Your word determines the kind of relationship you will enjoy with your fellowmen. It does not have the freedom and flexibility made possible by the telephone with its sanctuary of distance, so dear to the hearing person at the eleventh hour. When you have committed yourself, by mail or in a previous visit, to come to a party, you come. Even if you are feeling particularly misanthropic that night. You may excuse yourself with a few days' advance notice, again by mail or in person, but you have to be mighty convincing when you explain to the host that Jeane Dixon has divulged the future to you—that on the night of the party you would feel terribly antisocial, therefore it would be wise if you stay away.

"Your number is 48," the girl behind the counter smiles sweetly and turns to the next customer. Sam hesitates, then shrugs and finds a seat close to the take-out counter.

Bright kid, this girl. She reacted as if there were nothing out of the ordinary when a customer grabs the order pad and places his own order. No doubt she is also a great believer of miracles, that somehow your deafness will disappear before your pizza is ready and the number, whatever it is, announced on the loudspeaker.

The pizza tastes cold but good. Sam settles back and watches with affection as Brian and Brenda finish their portions. He waits until Jane returns with the coffee before waving for the family's attention. "Want to go to the lake next week?" he more announces than asks with his hands and fingers. Shrieks of delight answer him, unheard.

In group discussions where you alone are deaf, you do not exist. Because you cannot present your ideas through a medium everyone is accustomed to, you are not expected, much less asked, to contribute them. Because you are deaf, they turn deaf. Just do what your parents, friends, fellow workers—who can hear—tell you; you will know soon enough as we go along. Yours is not to reason why; yours is to do and die silently. Does no one realize that security comes from knowing what you will be doing next, knowing what to expect? Does no one agree that much of the joy of performing an activity stems from the realization that you had a hand in planning it?

"Yes, you may bring Barb and Jo along," Sam smiles as Brenda hugs the dolls and skips happily out of the room. To his seven-year-old son, he asks, "Brian, tell me, what can we do at the lake?"

You never forget that frightening experience. When you were Brian's age. You were left out of the dinner table conversation. It is called mental isolation. While everyone is talking or laughing, you are as far away as a lone Arab on a desert that stretches along every horizon. Everyone and everything are a mirage; you see them but you cannot touch or become a part of them. You thirst for connection. You suffocate inside but you cannot tell anyone of this horrible feeling. You do not know how to. You get the impression nobody understands or cares. You have no one to share your childish enthusiasm and curiosity, no sympathetic listener who can give meaning to your world and the desert around you. You are not granted even the illusion of participation. You are expected to spend 15 years in the strait-jacket of speech training and lipreading. You learn not how to communicate, only how to parrot words, never to speak your own. Meantime your parents never bother to put in an hour a day to learn the sign language or some part of it. One hour out of twenty-four that can change a lifetime for you. Instead, the most natural form of expression for you is dismissed as vulgar. It has never occurred to them that communication is more than method or talk. That it is a sense of belonging, an exchange of understanding, a mutual respect for the other's humanity.

The kids have been put in bed. Sam pours a third cup of coffee for himself. Jane is doing the dishes and he decides to get his pipe from the living room. He cannot find it and returns to the kitchen.

Your eyes are your contact with the world, but there is only so much you can see. Seeing is waiting. From the living room you cannot ask Jane about the pipe. In the kitchen you cannot ask while she is washing the carving knife. She cannot answer until the knife is safely put down. You must stop with half of the shaving lather still on your face to answer how you want your eggs done. Then Jane must hurry back to the kitchen before the waffle burns. You always have laryngitis when you call Brian and Brenda to supper. It is rude to notice the fly in your pie while Jane is talking. You must walk across the room and touch her shoulder if you want her attention. Or stamp on the floor and probably ruin her mood or concentration for the next half hour.

He almost spills the coffee. "Sorry, honey," Jane smiles.

"Did Bill come to the plant to see you?" she asks. Sam nods and adds, "And he was sore like a wounded bear." He takes two cubes of sugar and stirs the coffee. He puts the spoon down. "It's about the latest federal grant for a project on some problems of the deaf," he explains. "Exactly what problems I don't know. Bill isn't sure either, but he does know who is going to head it."

It is always someone with the magic prefix "Dr." before his name or some connection with some prestigious but distant institution. Someone Bill has run across at a recent workshop and asked:

"Have you had any practical experience, say teaching, in the field of 'deaf education'?"

"No."

"Have you had any professional connection with a residential school for the deaf or some large day class for the deaf?"

"No."

"Do you know a deaf person personally?"

"No."

"In your professional capacity, have you ever worked with a deaf person, this person being either an associate or subordinate?"

"No."

"Have you ever been to a club for the deaf, or some social gathering of the deaf?"

"No."

"Do you socialize with the deaf?"

"No."

"Have you ever spent a night in a discussion or chat with a deaf person?"

"No."

"In this workshop, do you integrate with deaf participants during the coffee breaks?"

"No."

"Did you try to?"

"No."

"Do you know how to communicate manually?"

"No."

"Do you believe the child should have a choice in methods of communication for the greatest stimulation of his intellectual growth?"

"No."

"One more question, sir. Would you attribute our failures in education and rehabilitating the deaf to a lack of understanding of the subject and his problems?"

"Yes. It's a damned shame. Let me tell you about this research I'm..."

Yes, it's a damned shame. Thanks to these armchair academicians, you find yourself cynical or apathetic toward the projects and programs that have been set up to improve your lot. Including those run by other professional people in the field, who are more open and honest, who have so rubbed elbows with you that their elbows ache if they do not move in a conversation with you. You are an American Indian resenting the white hearing man far away in some ivy-covered Indian Bureau, who has never laid his eyes on you but feels himself nevertheless qualified to declare what is wrong with you and to dictate your destiny.

Or you are too preoccupied in your struggle for a happy and meaningful life to give a hoot about these projects and programs. More than the hearing person, you need all the extra time you can get to achieve any ambitious goal. Yet you are expected by your own kind, by the "deaf intellectuals", to sacrifice this extra time to the cause of the deaf image, to help your less fortunate deaf brothers. You may even be expected to change jobs for one in which you can carry a larger part in this holy mission. You are under constant pressure to behave only in a manner favorable to this image.

The man on the tube looks as if he has a goldfish flipping inside his mouth. He refuses to leave; another joins him, mouthing likewise. Sam sighs and reaches for the channel dial. In a split second the Shakespeare Special is replaced by an undersea scene.

A big fish approaches the diver. Barracuda? It is going to attack the diver, or is it? Why does it hesitate, then swim off? What did the diver do that was not visibly obvious? Would he be attacked had he

*acted otherwise? But is the damn fish some kind of shark? The com-
mentator supplies all the answers but they pass through you as if you
were a sieve. Desperately you grab for what you can but you cannot
see what you cannot hear. A wealth of information, both practical and
exotic, escapes you daily. Television, movies and the stage hold limited
meaning for you. Radio, phonographs, tape recorders and loudspeakers
have none. Then to what do you turn for information? The nearby
human being is too unreliable. So you have only books. Read twice,
thrice, four times, as much as the average person to know just as
much. Slowly you close the cultural gap that is widening even faster
by the incredible speed and ease of modern media.*

Sam is alone in the living room, illuminated by a single
lamp. Jane has long since retired but he himself feels no ur-
gency for sleep. From the coffee table he picks up Remarque's
All Quiet on the Western Front. Hardly has he opened the book
before he reaches for the dictionary.

*What are haricot beans? Mess-tin? Dollop? Voracity? Already
four words out of your vocabulary, all from the first paragraph on the
first page! You read this classic as an adult while others read it in
their teens. You are lucky you can recognize the words as English. For
some deaf adults they might well be reading the original version in
German. Others with a little more reading ability plod through page
by page, this laborious effort dimming the brilliant power of the message and the brutal grace of the story. In addition, there are unfamiliar
idioms, colloquialisms, and expressions. The difficult language which
you have never mastered makes for difficult reading. As if it is not
enough, you lack the background information necessary for comprehension of the subject. Scratch out another—or your last—reliable
source of information.*

Finishing a chapter, he puts the book down and closes the
edge-torn dictionary. He rubs his eyes and stretches his arms.
The *Tribune* comes in his field of vision and he opens it to the
classified ads section.

*Maybe there's something you overlooked earlier tonight... Yes,
here's a possibility... Damn it, no address, just a lousy phone number... Have you enough of the job at the plant! Eight years of brain-
numbing drudgery. Is one such a coward not to quit? When you con-
template a job change, you are not half as concerned about the new*

location, working condition, fringe benefits, school for your children, new friends, etc., as you are about basic survival and a decent income that will permit your family to live in relative comfort. You don't move on because you itch for a change of scenery or because your boss doesn't like the length of your hair. You do not doubt your ability to change jobs, to perform the job or to keep the job, only whether you would be given a chance to prove this ability, to convince the prospective but skeptical employer that ability is all that counts. You can't write or read well. You can't speak. How do you sell yourself, by drawing pictures? All things being equal, the job goes to the applicant whose ears do not just hold up his eyeglasses.

Against the vast black nothingness a flect of light winks here and there, like distant planets greeting a lost traveler. Watching through the window, Sam suddenly realizes how much he loves the city.

In one city you dare not hope for many job openings, any kind, where the deafness of a worker is treated as irrelevant or routine. You may have to cross a dozen city limits, perhaps half a continent, before you find one. Then the lesser factors take on new importance. Such as Brian and Brenda's new playmates. The slow and often painful acceptance. The children are still learning to live with their and your handicap. Then there is the search for housing in want ads which seem to conspire against you, listing only phone numbers for the most desirable and reasonably priced units. And the orientation of local merchants and new neighbors to your deafness. And the deaf population in the new city which may turn out to consist entirely of your family. You are well settled here. Need you push your luck?

Slowly he folds the paper and gets up. He switches the lamp off and walks cautiously down the dark hall. His hands move along the wall, keeping in contact for balance which has been affected when he became deaf. At he door of his bedroom he pauses. As his eyes adjust to the darkness, he can make out the features of Jane's face.

Sam, do you love her or are you merely fond of her? You married her because she was available, the best of a limited lot. Probably she had said "Yes" for the same reason. It has always been this way: You don't have a ghost of a choice. Education, ambition, job, wife, friends, recreation, and sometimes religion. For you, choice is a limited word. You are the novelist's delight, the lonely, soul-searching character who has never found what he seeks in life. Unlike the perennial wanderer, you know which road you want to travel but you keep running into one roadblock or another. The day you lost your hearing your universe shrank many times over; your power of choice in a world of sound is drastically reduced. Thrown in the storm of silence, you seek refuge among your own kind and become a part of a microcosm which you are not sure you want. It is a closed society whose bond among members is founded not on mutual interests or intellectual equality, but on a common desire for escape from the "cruel outside world," for communication although this communication frequently turns out to be an illusion. It breeds dependence, stagnation, pettiness and finally boredom. It is a microcosm that unmercifully tries your individuality. You either surrender to tribal conformity or return to the other world. Or live on the fringes of both worlds, never to fully accept one and never to be fully accepted by the other.

He tosses in the bed. Unable to sleep, he stares at the far corner of the room. Jane stirs but is still again. He moves his hands to the back of his head and folds them.

Are you indulging in excessive self-pity? Brood and brood until there is no objectivity left in you? Is that why psychologists analyze you as being self-centered, immature, suspicious and narrow-minded, always self conscious and defensive about your inability to hear? An unhealthy mental attitude? Or shall we call it inevitable? This outlook is not a product of deafness per se but of a general public attitude, or ignorance, to the nature of deafness and the problems it creates.

Imagine yourself in a living room full of people who all know what is going on. Except you, who inquire and are answered with a polite smile which only underlines your helplessness. Everyone seems relaxed, enjoying himself. Except you, who are uneasily waiting for something to happen which makes sense to you. Everyone chats congenially with one another. Except you, who receive more polite smiles and fugitive glances. Everyone tells something hilarious and laughs. Except you who debate with yourself whether you would appear less ridiculous going along and laughing at Godknowswhat or remaining stoic thus making your deafness even more conspicuous in an atmosphere already made uneasy by your presence.

Leaving the room means crawling back into your "deaf shell" from which you seek escape in the first place. A triumph of futility. So you stay on, making the best of your dilemma, waiting, hoping for the breakthrough when someone will realize you are indeed human. And tolerance may yet become acceptance.

You find it difficult to forget for a moment you are deaf when you are continuously reminded by an unwitting public. You are daily subjected to this public's unpredictable reaction and to the necessity of proving yourself. A lifetime of unending strain. After all this, can you kid yourself about not becoming oversensitive in your human relationships?

You know you are getting a raw deal but you do not know whom to blame. Public ignorance is a faceless enemy against whom you have no weapon, only your battle-weary ingenuity. How do you get a society to accept you when it is ruled by this enemy? It can be educated to show understanding, compassion, but it does not always listen. Sometimes you wonder why it seems to be afraid of you.

People are, however, not your raison d'etre. Each unpleasant episode with them is an unavoidable skirmish. They represent only obstacles in your battle. The objective of the battle is a life in which you can sing between dejections, laugh between tears, and dream between nightmares. Breathe between repressions, love between prejudices, and grow between defeats. And, by God, you are making it.

Peace settles over Sam. He falls asleep with his arms around Jane.

6

It's Our World Too!

Ben Bahan

ON MY drive down to visit my parents, I was thinking about what topic to write about for this month's *Deaf Community News.*. For a while I panicked because I thought "this is it, I have reached the end of the tunnel. No more stories can be wrung out of my head." I'm telling you that's a disturbing feeling. I know I don't need to go through this, because many psychologists who claim to have expertise in how the deaf mind operates, have said that deaf people are emotionally disturbed beyond recuperation (Hofey, 1988). So, do you think I need this situation to pile up on my already "labeled state of mind"? No! So there was a desperate reason to panic.

I know you would never believe this, but what actually saved me was a *cockroach*! Let me tell you how this began.

About half way, I stopped at a roadside diner. A waitress was taking my order. I pointed to the menu. She went on and talked. Maybe she was telling me today's special. Anyway, I interrupted and gestured, "I can't hear," and went on pointing out my order.

She looked a bit irritated, and said, "Why don't you speak?" while pointing to her lips.

I thought "she must be one of those wackos," and proceeded to squirm my slimy tongue around its oral cavity and uttered, "Un hs..hagmerbersugar uth kees."

Reproduced by permission of the author and *Deaf Community News*.

She suddenly looked bewildered, and turned to look at the menu. She took my order and left.

Fifteen minutes later she came back with my cheeseburger and a note. I read the note and it said: "I have a deaf brother who went to wonderful school up north. Now he speeks wel, you know you shoold lern to speek. Its nevar to lat. Aftar al you lif in a hearing wurld."

I read her note and wondered where she learned to write. But as I read on, I thought, "what right does she have to claim, without asking me, that I did not receive speech training. After all, I went to a school that incorporates this method in its School Philosophy. Not to mention I spent countless hours of drills on how to say the sound P instead of B. Which, according to the philosophy, will enable me to successfully interact in the "Hearing World."

I was so infuriated by the note that I didn't realize she stood there waiting for my response.

As our eyes met, I saw her pupils dilate, and her mouth gaped in apparent horror. She backed off and ran to the kitchen. I touched my mouth to see if I was foaming like a mad dog with rabies. (Unfortunately I wasn't.) She returned with a can of Raid. I got up and quickly ran to defend myself, thinking, "What did I do to deserve getting sprayed by Raid." As she ran near me, I bent down and covered my face, only to discover she kept on running past me to the table that was directly behind my chair. There was a big cockroach crawling on the table. She must have sprayed more than half the can before it finally succumbed.

I just watched the whole scene in amazement. Naturally, I couldn't finish the cheeseburger. Who knows what happened in the kitchen? I just paid the bill and left a tip and split the joint as fast as I could. Of course, I tucked the note she wrote into my coat pocket.

On the road I returned to my dilemma (what to write about?) When I pulled out the note, I read it again. (That's something I don't encourage you to do: to read and drive at the same time; however the note was short.) The second time around, the one thing that hit me was the phrase: *it is a hearing world*.

I pondered on that issue. What right do hearing people have to impose on us the dominance of their world? What is even worse, there are deaf people who strongly uphold hearing world values on us deaf people. They go around saying you have to learn how to speak because it is a hearing world. It's strange because while they use that phrase, they are denying their own existence as a deaf person. If the world is not theirs, then who are they?

I am proposing for us all to go out and say, "Hell, it's our world, too! Of course, I cannot deny the fact that there are many more hearing people than there are deaf. But, I can and will deny them the right to claim the world. I, as a deaf person, have my own rights, my own place on this planet. Now, to go around and say "it is a hearing world" is a self-defeating prophecy. It does mean one thing: when we accept that quote we are lowering our standards of living into those of a puppet. We are what we are, signing people who function equally in every aspect of living.

There are hearing people, who have doctoral degrees in the education of the deaf/hearing impaired, going about teaching the fact that the deaf people are outnumbered. Therefore, they say we should adhere to the values of the majority (hearing world). They are poisoning the minds of the deaf children they teach, and it is those children that grow up into deaf adults. Then the adults go about telling others and me, that we have to learn to speak because it is a hearing world. Come to think of it, it is the very world they speak about that is dividing us, in the sense of united we stand divided we fall.

I ask you again, what right do hearing people and deaf people have to say it is a hearing world?

If we go about saying it is our world, too, we will show that we have a foothold in this place. It is those hearing people who will have to share the space with us, and if they want to, they are damn welcome to our world. But they must respect our needs to communicate in sign language . Because through sign language we learn everything about the world, its evil, its goodness, its ugliness and its beauty. What will we ever learn if we adhere to the speaking values? We get blinded by squinting our eyes and lipreading the two dimensional aspect of life.

By gaining our place, we must teach hearing people sign language. That way we are bridging the two worlds together. It won't ever work the other way around. It will never work!

I was already on Tappan Zee Bridge before I realized I had a story. I was wondering, "Really, who's world is it, anyway?" Yes, it belongs to all of us. But, I can't help wondering if there was anyone or anything that controls the world more than we do. Suddenly, a scene I faced two hours before appeared before me. If anyone or anything owns the world it's the cockroaches! It's their world, it's not the hearing people's world. They own the globe; there are people everywhere that either try to kill them (but end up finding out the cockroaches multiply), or worship them. And in the event of nuclear war, who survives? Cockroaches.

So is it a hearing world? No, it's a cockroach world! They rule the earth!

7

Dimensions of Difference: ASL and English Based Cultures

William C. Stokoe

When George L. Trager and Edward T. Hall and their colleagues in wartime Washington forty years ago set about isolating the basic units of culture they hit upon an ingenious scheme for recording the main outlines of any culture. They first identified ten "primary message systems" or isolates, and then examined each of the ten in relation to each of the other nine and to itself. The result, "A Map of Culture," is a grid or matrix of one hundred cells. (The map is reproduced here, by permission, from Hall's (1959) book, *The Silent Language*).

The names of the lines of the map are all abstract nouns, and the ten of them together, though they may not cover everything under the sun, do cover much of the "area" of a culture; that is, the business of life as people in all cultures live it. Because abstractions must be discovered, reached, or postulated by the working of mental processes, it is not difficult to see that whatever may be taken as an abstract entity, a thing in itself (e.g. *defense*) may equally well be taken as an aspect or a quality (i.e. defensive, or *protective*) of itself or of something else.

A Map of Culture

Primary Message Systems	Interactional	Organizational	Economic	Sexual
	0	1	2	3
Interaction	Communication Vocal qualifiers Kinesics Language	Status and Role	Exchange	How the sexes interact
0	00	01	02	03
Association	Community	Society Class Caste Government	Economic roles	Sexual roles
1	10	11	12	13
Subsistence	Ecological community	Occupational groupings	Work Formal work Maintenance Occupations	Sexual division of labor
2	20	21	22	23
Bisexuality	Sex community (clans, sibs)	Marriage groupings	Family	The Sexes Masc. vs. Fem. Sex (biological) Sex (technical)
3	30	31	32	33
Territoriality	Community territory	Group territory	Economic areas	Men's and women's territories
4	40	41	42	43
Temporality	Community cycles	Group cycles	Economic cycles	Men's and women's cyclical activities
5	50	51	52	53
Learning	Community lore—what gets taught and learned	Learning groups—educational institutions	Reward for teaching and learning	What the sexes are taught
6	60	61	62	63
Play	Community play—the arts and sports	Play groups—teams and troupes	Professional sports and entertainment	Men's and women's play, fun, and games
7	70	71	72	73
Defense	Community defenses—structured defense systems	Defense groups—armies, police, public health, organized religion	Economic patterns of defense	What the sexes defend (home, honor, etc.)
8	80	81	82	83
Exploitation	Communication networks	Organizational networks (cities, building groups, etc.)	Food, resources, and industrial equipment	What men and women are concerned with and own
9	90	91	92	93

A MAP OF CULTURE

Territorial 4	Temporal 5	Instructional 6	Recreational 7	Protective 8	Exploitational 9
Places of interaction 04	Times of interaction 05	Teaching and learning 06	Participation in the arts and sports (active and passive) 07	Protecting and being protected 08	Use of telephones, signals, writing, etc. 09
Local group roles 14	Age group roles 15	Teachers and learners 16	Entertainers and athletes 17	Protectors (doctors, clergy, soldiers, police, etc.) 18	Use of group property 19
Where the individual eats, cooks, etc. 24	When the individual eats, cooks, etc. 25	Learning from working 26	Pleasure from working 27	Care of health, protection of livelihood 28	Use of foods, resources, and equipment 29
Areas assigned to individuals by virtue of sex 34	Periods assigned to individuals by virtue of sex 35	Teaching and learning sex roles 36	Participation in recreation by sex 37	Protection of sex and fertility 38	Use of sex differentiating decoration and adornment 39
Space Formal space Informal space Boundaries 44	Scheduling of space 45	Teaching and learning individual space assignments 46	Fun, playing games, etc., in terms of space 47	Privacy 48	Use of fences and markers 49
Territorially determined cycles 54	Time Sequence Cycles Calendar 55	When the individual learns 56	When the individual plays 57	Rest, vacations, holidays 58	Use of time-telling devices, etc. 59
Places for learning 64	Scheduling of learning (group) 65	Enculturation Rearing Informal learning Education 66	Making learning fun 67	Learning self-defense and to stay healthy 68	Use of training aids 69
Recreational areas 74	Play seasons 75	Instructional play 76	Recreation Fun Playing Games 77	Exercise 78	Use of recreational materials (playthings) 79
What places are defended 84	The When of defense 85	Scientific, religious, and military training 86	Mass exercises and military games 87	Protection Formal defenses Informal defenses Technical defenses 88	Use of materials for protection 89
Property— what is enclosed, counted, and measured 94	What periods are measured and recorded 95	School buildings, training aids, etc. 96	Amusement and sporting goods and their industries 97	Fortifications, armaments, medical equipment, safety devices 98	Material Systems Contact w/ environment Motor habits Technology 99

A necessary consequence of this freedom to look at a domain of life both as a thing in itself and as an aspect of other domains, is that each category, when focused on itself, highlights a major area. Thus the cells in the diagonal line (00 to 99), their labels printed in boldface type, have a special importance.

If one makes a table of numbers and uses multiplication instead of noun modification by adjective as operation, the special nature of the resulting diagonal is apparent; the numbers in the diagonal are the perfect squares.

	1	2	3	4	...
1	1	2	3	4	
2	2	4	6	8	
3	3	6	9	12	
4	4	8	12	16	...

Anyone familiar with cultural description will see that what Hall has called the primary message systems are biological essentials, of all, not just human, life. In that sense they are certainly primary. What makes them message systems is what Hall's book is about: the way that people read meaning into the actions of others.

From his wide experience both in other cultures and in training Americans to work for government or business abroad, Hall fills his book, written for the layman as he says, with examples of how the messages taken as the normal nature of things within a culture, when sent silently across cultures, lead to misunderstanding, and how the misunderstanding may lead to loss of face, to loss of business, or even to an unpleasant international incident. But Hall's book is intended to do more than make diplomatic and commercial communication across cultures smoother. It has the larger purpose of showing that in each of these areas all that we take as normal—as "the way things are"—are behaviors determined by our culture; so determined, in fact, that we are sure that they are "normal" and invevitable. But this is not the case; in other cultures than our own, quite different, sometimes even opposite, behaviors are the norm.

Primary message systems and their differences, even between quite similar cultures, are often used for comic effect. Much of the well deserved success of the Crocodile Dundee films comes from clever exploiting of these differences. In Dundee's rugged outdoor society, "language, kinesics (gestures and facial expressions), and vocal qualifiers" (tone of voice and other vocal characteristics)—all these features of Cell 00 of Figure 1, along with the messages sent by clothing and hair style, signal categorically that a person one meets is either a man or a woman. Fooled once by the contradictory signals in American urban culture, Dundee seeks primary evidence directly, and finds he's got the message wrong again.

Conversely, in "Dragnet," a film that makes high camp of the generation-old Sgt. Friday radio and television series, the film's use of contrasting message systems almost fails. Young Joe Friday's new partner shows up in the garb of a '60s commune (or an '80s street person): head wrapped, riotous beard, ragged clothing, dirty feet poking out of scuffed sandals—a mess. Detective Sgt. Friday nearly gags but quotes him the police department's dress code. The film cuts at once to the partners getting into their unmarked car; but now Friday's partner, in coat and tie and neatly barbered, looks so different that the viewer fails for a time to realize that his partner is in fact the hippie of the previous scene.

Of course most of the multitude of signals being sent constantly in the primary message systems by every action of everyone are less laugh provoking or spectacular. The mismatch of signals across cultures or subcultures may make for high comedy—or for incidents that can lead to the brink of war, as Hall was well aware.

The two incidents from film just cited involve clothing, a most important way in any culture that messages are sent. The map locates clothing in the way that materials are exploited (Exploitational) for any of the ten rows. In examining differences between Deaf American culture (DAC) and Mainstream American culture (MAC) , it is convenient to start, as we have here, with the material end of the rows because the materials of a culture are among the first differences to strike the newcomer's eye.

This is not to suggest, however, that "material culture" is equivalent to "culture" or is more important than "cognitive culture." Cognitive culture, those maps and plans of life that are strikingly similar for all who possess a common culture, is what the Hall map attempts to make plainer. Indeed, the work of Hall and Trager and their group foreshadowed later developments in cognitive anthropology. I begin with exploitation of materials here simply because in this area the evidence is so easily seen.[1] Having begun there, we continue:

At Cell 09 ("Use of telephones, signals, writing, etc."), it is possible to note that there has been a marked difference between DAC and MAC ever since Alexander Graham Bell invented the telephone. Not many decades after his invention, a telephone in every (hearing) home became a visible mark of urban culture. Hearing people use telephones and think it a great misfortune if they must get along without them. Deaf people cannot use ordinary telephones and often hate the instant interruptions of their already scrappy interaction with hearing people. Indeed, use of the phone is a razor's-edge test of membership and acceptance in the Deaf community: those with a hearing loss who use the phone may be classed by others as "Hard of hearing" but never "Deaf (like us)." (I use the typographical distinction *deaf* vs. *Deaf* throughout to distinguish hearing impairment from cultural membership.)

The contrast between Bell's professed intention of helping the deaf and the effect of his invention is profound. The telephone isolated all those who were profoundly deaf, while it helped some of those whose hearing loss could be partially restored by louder and louder sound introduced into the ear. The telephone also changed the world and built fortunes, and these fortunes endowed foundations that often still insist on making deaf people hear or learn to act as if they could. The

---

1 See Carol Padden, this volume.

telephone linked hearing people together in ever expanding communication networks even as it excluded those who could not hear.

Time has given another twist to the irony, however. When Weitbrecht, a profoundly deaf engineer, perfected his acoustic coupler in the 1960s, teletype machines (and later newer devices no bigger than a desk telephone), with ordinary phone handsets pressed into cups, could produce distinctive patterns of beeps to be picked up in the microphone as each key on one device's keyboard was touched, and could transform these beeps into the character display (or printer) on the device at the other end of the phone line. After a century of exclusion, deaf people and the Deaf community can now benefit from the electronic technology that the genius of one deaf man spliced into the world wide telephone network.

The use of time-telling devices (Cell 59), another difference in the exploitation of materials, is so familiar in MAC that the uninitiated to DAC are startled by deaf people's alarm clocks, which flash a light instead of making sounds. But the main dimension of difference, **the use of vision instead of hearing for getting vital and incidental information,** is the fundamental difference between MAC and DAC, and it shows up in every cell of the Hall map as one explores DAC.

To calibrate the map for DAC and all other Deaf cultures, it is best to begin in the key Cell, 00. Its label, "Communication, Vocal qualifiers, Kinesics, Language," needs a minor change, to: "Communication, Pantomime, Gesture, Language." The change of only two of the terms may look slight, but it is of the utmost importance.

If the interactional aspect of human interaction is communication in its broadest sense, language is communication at its most organized. In all hearing cultures, "vocal qualifiers" "kinesics" ("tone of voice" and "gesticulation" in ordinary parlance) send messages that usually accompany the use of language but often occur alone. For members of a Deaf culture interacting face to face, a signed language will usually be the means of interaction; but when deaf persons communicating do not possess a sign language in common, their practiced use of pantomime and *ad hoc* gesture make communication possible.[2]

In the next diagonal cell, "Society, Class, Caste, Government," the difference between a national culture and a special culture[3] becomes clear. The government of general American culture is "the government," which is the government of Deaf Americans as well. Otherwise, however, there is another dimension of difference here. Sociologists have for a long time been interested in the American deaf community, and their descriptions cover some of the area of several cells around Cell 11, especially Cell 31. Marriage groupings give striking evidence of cultural as well as sociological diffference: more than 90% of deaf persons marry other deaf persons, and deaf women with hearing husbands are more numerous than deaf men with hearing wives.[4]

Sociological studies of deaf society can be mapped onto the map of culture, but they are not usually undertaken or understood as cultural or ethnographic studies; i.e. as studies of social organization in a different culture. Hall emphasizes throughout *The Silent Language* the systematic and total nature of culture. He warns of the danger in a mode of thought that ignores difference in logical types—between social institutions and a culture. Institutions like marriage, law, and schools are components of culture and differ from culture to culture. Deaf Americans, who marry one another, who form their own clubs and associations, and who interact largely with their own kind, are seen erroneously by some sociologists as Americans with a physical impairment, a disability, a handicap, who have not been able to achieve the full status accorded to hearing persons.

---

2 See Battison and Jordan, 1976.

3 The term "subculture" suggests inferiority to those unfamiliar with cultural anthropology; hence the term "special culture." However it is designated though, the culture under discussion is included in a larger culture, which nevertheless cannot interpenetrate it. Although the Deaf community contains as little as one one-thousandth of the total community, the respective languages and cultures influence one another in only relatively minor ways.

4 Best, Lunde, etc.

Deaf Americans may not be able to hear, but they are people who cope with life, with the ten primary message systems common to all cultures, and with the whole area the map covers. They do so in ways that are different, not better or worse. Sociological studies of "deafness" often miss this most important point.

Up, down, and right one Cell from 11, in "Status and Role" and "Occupational groupings" and "Economic roles," other sharp differences between DAC and MAC surface. It is often said that in American society the possession of wealth or a large income plays a large part in status, but be that as it may, in Deaf society, money and even education may be subordinate to other status-conferring factors. A highly educated deaf person may not share the culture or use the language centeral to DAC. Such a person, however, is at risk. Those who "pass" in the hearing world may be able to move between the two cultures. The late Ben Schowe, a deaf man himself, has written a book about these exceptional ones (Schowe 1979). These deaf people successful in finding a niche in MAC are rare individuals as Schowe emphasizes; many others who attempt it fail to achieve full membership in either culture, because they cannot communicate freely and comfortably with either hearing or deaf others (Stokoe, Bernard, & Padden 1976).

At the center of the map, the metaphysical yet inescapable abstractions, Time and Space, serve to remind us that students of Deaf culture have given little attention to territorial differences. Living space—where one lives, rents, or owns a home—is of course subject to the patterns of Mainstream American Culture: income, occupation, and other factors help define limits, but within them, in DAC, there are special and different patterns worth study.[5] Deaf people tend to be more thickly represented in urban than in rural populations in America, but their tendency to live in the same neighborhood

---

5 Simon Carmel, a deaf anthropologist, has described three social clubs of the Deaf in an American industrial city; like all such clubs, their members are Deaf of course, but they also follow MAC patterns, in being respectively Black, White Blue- Collar, and White White-collar in makeup.

as other Deaf people has yet to be carefully studied. "Places of interaction" (Territorial cell 04) have received attention because Deaf clubs are obvious gathering places, as are churches with Deaf congregations, but this attention has not often included ethnographic scrutiny.

Cell 15, "Age group roles," and Cell 32, "Family," also mark off areas where DAC and MAC differ strikingly, and the literature on deafness is full of references, often pejorative, to the dimensions of difference in these areas. Because only four or five out of one hundred children with hearing loss sufficient to destine them for DAC are born into hearing families, their enculturation, like their language acquisition and their education, is unusual both in time and rate. For most of those who become fully enculturated as Deaf, the school and not the family has been the primary formative influence. Consequently, there is little interaction between deaf youngsters and Deaf adults, until the former have reached and passed school leaving age. Indeed, there may be a long interval before the young deaf person makes contact with the Deaf community and begins attending the local club, finding fairly stable employment, meets and marries a Deaf spouse.[6]

It is time to stop, despite the temptation to look in many cells of the map for dimensions of difference. The purpose here has been not to define the dimensions but to suggest that Hall's map provides an excellent tool for discovering them. By careful perusal of the whole map, by seeking to understand fully all that the terse cell labels cover, the student of Deaf American Culture can find just those areas in which his or her major interest lies. It is possible that in any one of the cells there is material for a dissertation or monograph comparing message systems in DAC and MAC. But if ethnographers of Deaf society were to consider all the rows and columns of the map, the work of many researchers in different areas could be combined to

---

6 Pierre Gorman, from Australia and the first deaf person to earn a degree from Cambridge, in his dissertation, chronicles the pattern of deaf school leavers in Britain: an average of 10 years in special schools, then an average of 10 years aimless drifting from job to job and social agency until they make contact with the Deaf community.

form a larger coherent picture, more or less in the manner of aerial photographic mosaics. When that happens the world may begin to respect Deaf persons and their language and culture as different, not inferior.

8

Our Future, Ourselves

Ben Bahan

I WAS talking with a friend about the future.

She asked, "Why worry about the future when we have enough problems to deal with today?"

She has a point, but many of today's problems were born yesterday. Many things I have put off doing before turned into problems later. Some of those problems could have been solved if I had begun to look into the future.

So I now consider myself an amateur futurologist.

For the same reasons the deaf community should focus on the future. We ignore many issues today that could become the problems of tomorrow.

We're not "perfect"

Technology has its miracles and monsters. I read an article about cochlear implants, with a picture of a smiling six-year-old girl with implants. This is evidence that people are willing to use technology to manipulate, or correct what they consider "wrong".

I see a goal in the scientific community to solve the "disease" they call deafness.

We have come to an era where we can create test-tube babies, through genetic engineering called cloning. We can

Reproduced by permission of the author and *Deaf Community News*.

create another Steve Nover by taking out one hair, a cell, and a strand of DNA which has the blueprint of his body.

Then we put this DNA information in a zygote which is the beginning stage of babies (after the sperm meets the egg), and presto! We have an exact copy of Steve Nover. This isn't fantasy—it's been done with a frog.

Someday scientists will correct the genes to make a "perfect" race of people. "Perfect" meaning people who hear. This is a major concern we have for the future; our evidence is here today with cochlear implants.

The commission's future

We should begin to think about other issues of the near future. While we should celebrate the passage of the law creating the Massachusetts Commission for the Deaf and Hard of Hearing, we should begin to think of the problems we might face. For example, there could be a disagreement over service priority between the deaf and hard-of-hearing, who each have different needs. When it comes to a limited budget, sacrifices will be made and not everyone will be happy.

I can see the commission fighting inter-bureaucratic wars between different government agencies like the Massachusetts Rehabilitation Commission when it comes to who does what, and who gets what (budget).

Finally, a gap might grow between the deaf and the disabled communities created by the forming of the commission.

These problems may never happen, but because they might we should be prepared to develop strategies now to avoid them later.

"Gimme, gimme"

After explaining this to my friend, she began to see I had a point and I looked into the future to tell her what I think Massachusetts School for the Deaf (MSAD) and all deaf people should be doing. We should start broadening our concerns. All along our concern has been deafness-related issues, which is understandable.

We should become concerned for our neighbors' well-being and ours. To do that we must improve our living conditions first—we are doing that—by being involved in legislative actions: creating the commission, passing the deaf rights bill, etc.

Now we must focus on broader issues. Should MSAD take a position on favoring Ted Kennedy's plans for nationalized (government) medical care? It affects many deaf people's lives; most of us aren't rich, nor are many of our working-class hearing neighbors.

Should we voice our concerns about the Social Security cuts that President Reagan wants to enact? Those cuts would affect us and our neighbors, too.

I told my friend she'd be surprised at how much support we'd get if we showed concern for others as well as ourselves, instead of going around saying, "gimme, gimme."

I even believe MSAD should state its position on nuclear weapons, saying we urge both the Soviet Union and the U.S. to work successfully towards disarmament. That way we show concern for all our neighbors in the world. She thought I was going crazy on this idea.

We must show concern

Two days later, while I watched President Reagan give his State of the Union address, my doorbell light began to flash. I thought, "What idiot would interrupt me now?"

I went to the door and a young man was there with a notebook. I told him I am deaf. He asked me if I could lipread.

I said, "Yes," hoping he had readable lips. He didn't.

After a few frustrating minutes we gave up. He opened his notebook and wrote, "We are seeking new members to join our cause for Nuclear Disarmament."

My friend may be right; I might be crazy, but I would have been understood and could have voiced my feelings fluently among MSAD members. It may not be our top priority, but the futurologist in me thinks that someday we will have to say something that concerns our existence on earth.

9

Funny in Deaf–Not in Hearing

Susan D. Rutherford

THERE IS an incident in the Broadway play, "Children of a Lesser God," that speaks directly to my subject. For the reader who may not be familiar with the play, the action concerns the relationship of James, a hearing man, and Sara, a Deaf[1] woman. At one point James boasts of how funny he is. Sarah snaps back her disagreement; "You're funny in hearing," she signs, "not in Deaf."

That one line reveals much—both about humor and about the two cultures I am concerned with here. The focus of this

Reproduced by permission of the American Folklore Society from *Journal of American Folklore,* 96:381, 1983. Not for further reproduction.

Parts of this paper were first presented at the American Folklore Society annual meeting in San Antonio, October, 1981 and at the California Folklore Society annual meeting at Davis, California, April 1982.

The author would like to gratefully acknowledge all of the people who contributed to the collection, discussion, and/or analysis of the texts, particularly Ben Bahan, Dr. Byron Burnes, Olin Fortney, Leo M. Jacobs, Freda Norman, Carlene Canady-Pederson, Marie Phillips, Lillian Quartermus, and Howie Seago. Special thanks go to Ella Mae Lentz whose guidance, support, and friendship has been invaluable to this "outsider."

[1]The capitalized "Deaf" will be used in this paper to designate the cultural group as opposed to the lower case "deaf," which refers to the audiometric condition of not being able to perceive the sounds of speech.

paper is on the text of a joke that reflects the other side of the coin—funny in Deaf, not in hearing.

Bascom taught us that "amusement is, obviously, one of the functions of folklore, and an important one; but even this statement cannot be accepted today as a complete answer, for it is apparent that beneath a great deal of humor lies a deeper meaning" (1965:285). My study of this text was based on the belief that through an examination of a community's folklore one can find a reflection of its culture, and it is perhaps through the humor of the group, and its unselfconscious release of anxieties, that can get closest to the essence of the community. As Dundes aptly puts it, "it is what makes people laugh that reveals the soul of the people" (1973:611).

The joke in question has a long history in the American Deaf community. Quite often it is the first joke cited when informants are asked for an example of a "deaf" joke. Further, it is often referred to as a joke hearing people would not understand. My discussion is based on 13 texts and informant analyses collected in American Sign Language (ASL) on video tape. The following is an English translation[2] of one collected text:

> One time a man, well a person, a Deaf person, was driving along and stopped at some train tracks because the crossing signal gates were down but there was no train going by. So he waited for a long time for a train to go by, but nothing. The person decided then to get out of the car and walk to the control booth where there was a man who controlled the railroad gates. He was sitting there talking on the phone. The Deaf man wrote in his very best way (elegantly), "Please b-u-t," and handed the paper to the controller. The controller looked back at the Deaf person quizzically, "Please but? Huh?" He didn't understand that.

Funny in Deaf not in hearing.

If you are a nonsigner, you would not find the joke funny at all. The punch line is a play on sign. There is a substitution of

---

[2]All translations of texts are my own.

one of the parameters of ASL, similar to the substitution of a letter in a spoken word that creates a play on that word.

ASL has four parameters that, together with certain non-manual components (facial expression, body posture, movement of the head, body and eyes), comprise the phonological system of that language. Just as in spoken language, the phonology represents the building blocks upon which the language is based.

The parameters of ASL are: (1) hand shape; (2) palm orientation; (3) movement; (4) place of articulation. We can see these illustrated, for example, in the sign for "candy" (see Fig. 1):

1. Hand shape /G/
2. Palm orientation: down
3. Movement: twist (as arrow indicates)
4. Place of articulation: cheek

Figure 1. "Candy" (used with the permission of Harvard University Press).

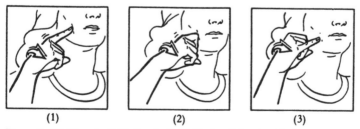

(1) (2) (3)

Figure 2. (1) "Candy," (2) "apple," (3) "jealous" (used with the permission of Harvard University Press).

The change in any one of these parameters can change the meaning of the sign. The signs for "apple" and "jealous" are the same as "candy" except for hand shape[3] (see Fig. 2)

The sign used by the informant for "open the railroad crossing gate" was the /G/ hand shape classifier, as follows, The movement resembles an actual crossing gate being raised and lowered. Note the palm orientation: it is inward, palms facing each other (see Fig. 3)

The ASL lexical equivalent for the English word "but" has the same parameters as the above classifier for railroad crossing gate, with the exception of palm orientation, as illustrated—the palms are facing outward (see Fig. 4).

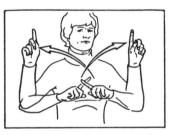

Figure 3. "Open the railroad crossing gates" (used with the permission of T. J. Publishers).

Figure 4. "But" (used with permission of T. J. Publishers).

Thus, the punchline, "Please b-u-t," is an obvious punlike play between the phonological similarities of the two signs. The play is on the intended idea: "Please, open the gate and let me pass." The substitution of the one phonological element of palm orientation would be similar to the substitutions in: "The Reverend Spooner had a great affection, or so he said, for 'our queer old dean'" (Koestler 1964:64).

Whether "Please b-u-t" is a true pun is debatable. There is a change in meaning from "open the railroad gates" to "but," however, the new statement does not make equal sense with the new meaning. A true pun would generally evoke a double

---

[3]For further discussion, see Klima and Bellugi (1978:417).

meaning with the phonological play where both meanings are perceived simultaneously. As we can see with the previous examples, "Our queer old dean" and "Our dear old queen," each statement makes sense. Compare this with the two meanings in the joke: "Please, open the railroad crossing gate," and "Please, b-u-t." The latter does not make equal sense.

The play is also one step removed. Since the person telling the joke writes the English word b-u-t, and does not use the sign "but," the play is actually with the English gloss.

But even many people who are fluent in sign and who understand and enjoy the play between sign and gloss do not fully appreciate the joke. That this happens is evidence of the more important fact of the cultural specificity of humor, for here, the lack of appreciation does not stem from "not getting it," but from a lack of a shared cultural experience. I was witness to a clear instance of this cultural difference at a workshop that I was conducting at a San Francisco Bay Area Deaf community service agency. The audience was mixed. There were Deaf people and there were hearing people. The hearing people included nonsigners, fluent signers, and native signers (children of Deaf parents). We were discussing culture, particularly Deaf culture, and I mentioned humor as being culturally specific. One of the participants asked if I would tell a Deaf joke. This is not my skill, but a Deaf friend—and master comedienne—consented. I include a translation of her text as one of the variations I collected:

> There is a Deaf man driving along in his car. He is hurrying to get home because his wife will get very angry if he is late. He then comes to a railroad crossing and the gates are down. He waits as the train passes. The train is long past and still the gates are down. The man waits and waits and is thinking of how his wife is going to yell if he's late. The Deaf man then gets out of his car and proceeds to the control booth at the crossing, where there is a person who is in charge of all the controls. The Deaf man takes out his pencil and paper and tries to think of the English words to put on the paper requesting that the gates be raised. He thinks and thinks (in sign) and says to himself, ah ha, and writes the words, "Please b-u-t," and hands the paper to the hearing

> gatekeeper. The gatekeeper does not understand and says, "Huh?"

Of the Deaf and hearing signers who understood the play on the sign, there was a definite qualitative difference in the laughter, which broke along Deaf and hearing lines. The Deaf response was much more intense.

Why the difference, especially since this is a very old joke and many of the Deaf individuals had heard it over and over again? Why funnier to Deaf than to hearing?

Consider again the cultural specificity of humor. The reason that humor is culturally specific for a group is more than just language; it is a matter of experience. It becomes clear that the one thing not held in common by the native hearing signers and the Deaf signers is the experience of being Deaf with all its cultural implications. The experience of being a Deaf person in the hearing world is one that is fraught with daily communication frustration, as well as societal prejudices and the collective oppression of Deaf people. These are not part of a hearing person's life experience. Hearing signers, through professional or familial ties, are generally aware to one degree or another of the frustrations and injustices Deaf people face. However, this awareness is usually on a more cognitive level, not on a deep, affective level.

Although a general level of awareness of deafness is increasing among the hearing world, it is not widely understood that there is a culture of Deaf people. It is a common misconception that Deaf people are an isolated, handicapped group of people. Whereas this may be the case for some, it is not the case for all. The American Deaf community is a group of deaf and hard-of-hearing individuals who share a common language and culture.[4] In the United States there are two million people who are "audiometrically deaf" (Schein and Delk 1974:17); that is, they are physically unable to perceive the sounds of speech. The Deaf community, however, numbers

---

[4]For additional discussion of the Deaf community as a cultural group, see Baker and Padden (1978), Baker and Battison (1980) Woodward (1982), Meadow (1972), Markowicz and Woodward (1975), Lunde (1960).

approximately 500,000. Membership in this cultural group is based more on "attitudinal deafness" (Baker and Padden 1978:1) than on the actual degree of hearing loss. By attitudinal deafness we mean that an individual has, on the basis of certain characteristics, identified himself as a member of the community and is accepted by other members.

The use of ASL is the major identifying characteristic of members of the Deaf Community (Stokoe 1970:27-41 and this volume). Thus, individuals who are deaf but do not use ASL are not considered members of the Deaf community.

Another cultural characteristic of the community is its 85-95 percent endogamous marriage rate (Rainer *et al.* 1963:17). Deaf people tend to marry other Deaf almost exclusively. Still another characteristic, the existence of a formal societal structure within the culture, can be seen in the numerous Deaf organizations—local, state, national, and international. Of particular note are the National Association of the Deaf (established in 1880) and The World Federation of the Deaf, which involve themselves with the problems of the deaf on national and international levels, respectively. There is also an American Athletic Association of the Deaf, which organizes Deaf sports and sends representatives to the World Deaf Olympics.

The Deaf community is a tight-knit one, and there are national fraternal orders, sororities and alumni associations, as well as numerous religious organizations and community social groups (Meadow 1972:24). There are articles of material culture such as telecommunication devices (TDDs) and flashing light signaling devices to take the place of doorbells, clock alarms, and telephone rings. There are even sound-activated signal lights to alert parents to a baby's cry.

Ten percent of the Deaf community's population are members of Deaf families whose principal language is ASL. The remaining 90 percent of the population are born to hearing families and are consequently potential members of a cultural group different from that of their own parents. State-operated residential schools for the deaf are the primary places where enculturation of these children takes place (Meadow 1972:24).

There, through peers from Deaf families and through Deaf adult staff, if present, this process is carried on—informally, often surreptitiously and without the official sanction of the educational establishment.

One important characteristic to note regarding this culture is that it is a bilingual diglossic community. Its members are a minority functioning within a larger society. Their language continuum ranges from ASL to English with many varieties of pidgin in between (Stokoe 1970:27; Woodward 1973:191). The "we" and "they" dichotomy of this minority group is roughly: "we" are Deaf, "they" are hearing: "we" identify with ASL, "they," English. [5]

If we look at the manifest content of the joke we see that the issue is one of communication or the lack thereof. It is also making fun of Deaf English.[6] Like the stilted expression of many whose knowledge of a second language is rudimentary, the language variety referred to as "Deaf English" is also characterized by simpler structure and over-generalization of the grammatical rules of English. For example, if "walk" becomes "walked," why then doesn't "go" become "goed"? If more than one "mouse" is "mice," why is the plural of "house" not "hice"? Another aspect of Deaf English is the substitution of the English gloss for an ASL sign. In the joke, the Deaf person is unable to find the right English words. In this case the right "words" are "open the railroad gate." Trying his or her best,

---

[5]The Deaf community has faced and continues to face the same kind of linguistic and cultural oppression as other minority groups. Without a voice in the decision-making process, self-determination for the community has been an impossibility. As Woodward (1982) points out, the Deaf community has three additional pressures that other minority groups do not have. First, there is the necessity to overcome the negative stereotype that accompanies a label of medical pathology. Secondly, the majority of the community's members are of a different cultural group than their parents and, thus, do not get cultural reinforcement in the home as do other minority children. And thirdly, the community's language differs in channel structure as well as code structure from that of the majority culture, which makes the language oppression doubly severe.

[6]For additional discussion of "Deaf English," see Meadow (1980) and Charrow (1975).

groping for the right words, the Deaf person falls into an English gloss of ASL sign, which is identical in all respects but one. The punlike play is between the phonological similarity of the two signs.

Although perhaps not a true pun, the joke does present one frame of reference, "open the railroad crossing gates," and then switches to another, "but," provoking what Koestler terms a bisociative act, as a true pun would. Koestler sees this bisociative act as "the perceiving of a situation or idea ... in two self-connected but habitually incompatible frames of reference" (1964:35). With the connecting of the dissimilar frames of reference an insight into the similarity between the two previously incompatible worlds is revealed. It is this resolution, according to Koestler, that makes us laugh or find something funny. It is my belief that two bisociative acts are at work here: one centering on ASL phonological similarity and the other on the English gloss substitution.

Of the informant analyses that went beyond the description of the play on sign, all referred to the Deaf person's problem with English. To quote a few: "The joke makes fun of Deaf people's English and their problems with writing"; "Deaf people always are having trouble with English"; "English is always a problem, you know that. So it's just a way of making fun of it."

One informant went further:

> You have to understand both languages in order to understand the joke. The joke makes fun of the Deaf person. You see Deaf people write down what they say. There are many possible English word choices. The Deaf person in the joke thinks what he/she wants to say in sign and then ends up writing English gloss. The Deaf person is writing so the hearing person can understand, but really, in sign it is not funny. The joke makes fun of Deaf English and the writing problems, which "they" blame on the influence of sign language. People blame sign language, so we have jokes that blame sign language. We laugh at that.

This is not only an insightful analysis, but a clear illustration of "we" and "they."

Herskovits reminds us that "the folklore of a people cannot be understood without an understanding of the culture to which it belongs" (1948:418). Considering how much of our socialization and education depend on language, we cannot understand the culture of Deaf people without understanding the educational system that controls the enculturation and linguistic development of the Deaf individual.

In 1837, after visiting a school for the deaf in Paris, a hearing minister, the Reverend Thomas Gallaudet, together with a French deaf teacher Laurent Clerc, established the first school for the deaf in America. Because the school they established was a residential one, deaf children who were previously isolated were able to gather together and form a community; this created the essential environment for the natural development of a language.

The educational approach that Gallaudet and Clerc used was called the "Combined Method." The children were schooled in the French Sign Language that the two men brought from France, as well as in speech.[7] In general, this combined oral and manual method was the standard approach in Deaf Education until the 1860s when the "oral Method" took hold.

The Oral Method's emphasis is on speech only. Sign language is forbidden both in and out of the classroom, since Oral proponents postulate that to allow signing would hinder a deaf person's development of speech. He would become lazy. The effort is to "normalize" a deaf child so he can be like a hearing person. In fact, a look at old Deaf Education texts reveals references to teaching the child to hear. Children who failed at the oral method were often thought to be stupid and would be sent to a Manual or Combined program. It was this shift to the oral method that began what some refer to as "The Hundred Years' War" or "The Oral-Manual Controversy."

---

[7]For further historical discussion see Lane (1977), Gannon (1980), and Bender (1970).

There had been an early acceptance of Deaf educators in Deaf Education in the mid-1800s. However, as the shift to oralism took hold this acceptance of Deaf teachers, as well as of Deaf administrators being involved in the decision-making process, began to wane. In fact, many of the Deaf schools that were founded by Deaf people gradually were taken over by hearing administrators.

By 1880, an International Conference of Teachers of the Deaf held in Milan, Italy, resolved to settle the Oral-Manual conflict. The following was the result:

> The congress, considering the incontestable superiority of speech over signing in restoring the deaf mute to society, and in giving him a more perfect knowledge of language, declares that the oral method ought to be preferred to that of signs for the education of the deaf and dumb.[Gordon 1892:xvi]

Notably, there were no Deaf persons in attendance or involved in drafting the resolution.

While the Oral-Manual struggle was going on, changes were taking place in the Deaf population. Medical advances were lessening the incidence of deafness due to childhood disease, while at the same time ensuring the survival of babies who were born deaf due to prematurity. The result was an increase in prelingually deaf children—those who become deaf before acquiring language. For the prelingually Deaf individual, the learning of spoken English is a particularly arduous task. Fant created an analogy for hearing people which is worth quoting:

> Suppose, for example, you were in a sound-proof, glass booth, equipped only with a pad and pencil. Outside the booth is your instructor who speaks, reads, and writes only Japanese. How long would it take for you to learn Japanese? How well would you learn it? [1972:v]

Orwell went so far as to say that if you control the language you control the people. When a people are dependent exclusively on a visual mode to acquire language, the suppression of a visual form of language is doubly oppressive. "Please b-u-t" is funny as a bilingual play, but again as Bascom asserts, "it is apparent that beneath a great deal of humor lies a deeper meaning" (1965:285). The deeper meaning here is a crystallized reflection of a historical and sociological experience of the Deaf. It is a picture of lack of control, lack of self determination, negation of identity, stifled development, blocked communication, external control characterized by benevolent paternalism and authoritarianism, and one of general conflict with the majority culture.

This joke, which has been described as an "old chestnut" by a senior member of the community, is also often referred to as "a joke hearing people wouldn't understand." In *Mother Wit from the Laughing Barrel*, Dundes states that "it is really in the in-group jokes and understanding that a group tests the solidarity of its members. Those who understand are 'with it'; those who do not understand are not 'with it'" (1973:611). With the explicit statement that a hearing person would not understand the joke, there is an overt definition of in-group/out-group—those who are "with it" and those who are not.

We know from the content of the joke that the gate controller is hearing, as the Deaf man must communicate with him through written notes. However, frequently within the telling there are embellishments such as depicting him in a derogatory fashion, talking on and on and occasionally indifferent to the Deaf man's presence. Just as Basso observes that in Western Apache folkloric tradition the portrayal of "'the Whiteman' serves as a conspicuous vehicle for conceptions that define and characterize what 'the Indian' is not" (1979:5), so we may suggest that the hearing man here serves the same purpose. This is especially true when the hearing man illustrates his indifference to Deaf people and his penchant for speech. In the joke frame, slurred images of hearing people are safely expressed. The aggression against the majority culture is safely masked by the humor.

Dundes suggests that "Sources of anxiety make the best subjects for humor," noting that "race prejudice is a common theme in Negro jokes" (1973:612). Similarly, "Please b-u-t" focuses on miscommunication and an ambiguous linguistic situation, both of which are daily sources of anxiety within the Deaf community. Dundes continues, "On the other hand, much humor is entirely intragroup rather than intergroup, and one often finds one Negro group making fun of another" (1973:612). As we have discussed earlier, informant analyses attest to the fact that "Please b-u-t" is also making fun of Deaf people and their misuse of English.

Martineau (1972) suggests that when the in-group humor is disparaging toward an out-group, as in the derogatory depictions of the hearing controller, it may serve to increase morale and solidify the in-group, and/or to introduce and foster a hostile disposition toward the out-group (1972:116). The former function is certainly fulfilled by this joke, and I would suggest that the latter is also a possible function for some of the tellers of this joke. Martineau also suggests four functions of in-group humor that is disparaging to the in-group: (1) to control in-group behavior; (2) to solidify the in-group; (3) to introduce or foster conflict already present in the group; and (4) to foster demoralization and social disintegration of the group. The latter two do not seem to be as relevant in this situation. Based on my observations and informant analyses, the first two functions do seem to have some validity. The joke-teller displays the proper behavior and attitude of the Deaf man in the joke, thus reaffirming group behavioral norms and attitudes. A common occurrence of Deaf and hearing interaction is dramatized, illustrating sources of mutual anxiety, and this serves to rally the group around a point of solidarity and demonstrate what is "Deaf" and what is not.

Douglas asserts that jokes mirror the incongruity in society. Jokes are antistructure—an attack on the established order. By joking in a play frame, the resultant disruption challenges the social order on a symbolic level and reaffirms order on a social level (1968:361).

Further, Feinberg suggests that word play is aggression against conformity, especially, with reference to puns, a rebellion against linguistic conformity. When the language is distorted, it represents a revolt, albeit playful, against the rigidity of language (Feinberg 1978:106). Given the history of linguistic rigidity imposed on the Deaf individual by the majority culture, it is apparent that "Please b-u-t," as a playful linguistic distortion, serves as a particularly satisfying source of rebellion. This is especially true for those who must walk daily the linguistic tightrope between both worlds.

In her paper, "The Social Control of Cognition: Some Factors in Joke Perception," Douglas, accepting Freud's analysis that the joke is an attack on control, states, "Since its form consists of a victorious tilting of uncontrol against control, it is an image of the leveling of hierarchy, the triumph of intimacy over formality and unofficial values over official ones" (1968:365). In the real world, the Deaf community has at least begun to level that hierarchy by identifying what it believes to be the major root of its problems. As one Deaf writer states, "Deaf people have been repressed, restrained and frustrated in their search for an adequate education and an equal opportunity for a meaningful life" (Jacobs 1981:2). The greatest handicap for the Deaf individual is not the inability to hear, but the ignorance of the hearing world. As Jacobs states, "many parents and educators fail to realize the critical need for communication" (1981:12).

"Please b-u-t" symbolically captures the essence of the Deaf situation perfectly: the gates block the way for the Deaf person's own good. It may be reasonable to expect such protection for a while, but the obstruction remains beyond a reasonable time. This parallels the experience of many Deaf individuals within the education system.

In control of the situation, of course, is a hearing person, often portrayed talking on the telephone and indifferent to the Deaf person's situation. This is perhaps as close to a Deaf stereotype of a hearing person as we can get.

Frustration mounts as the Deaf person's way continues to be blocked. He is expected to arrive home no matter what, or his authoritarian wife will be angry. The Deaf person is caught: he has to play the game the hearing way, which for him carries built-in failure, but at the same time he is expected to succeed.

This double-bind situation aggravates the frustration and erodes the self-esteem of the individual.

When he gives the hearing gatekeeper the written English note, the gatekeeper does not understand. It should be noted here that speech therapists often tell a deaf child how well he speaks. While the child may be relatively proficient in the realm of Deaf speech, it is not uncommon that in the outside world the child will be unable to make his speech understood. The majority culture—the hearing world—does not understand him.

The Deaf person in the joke, as one informant states, "writes his very best" and is still not understood. The slap at hearing control and education is obvious. The Deaf person does his best to communicate as the hearing world has taught him, but communication breaks down. It is, however, a key point, underlining Jacobs's point about an uninformed hearing world, that it is the hearing gatekeeper who fails to grasp the true situation.

The joke serves a second purpose, which sheds light on another source of anxiety. Since this joke is for the bilingual, it may serve as an additional source of group solidarity and identification for those who have to interact with the hearing world more than their more isolated fellows (who may not have an equal grasp of English). The greater the command of English a Deaf individual has, the more likely he is to be in conflict with himself.

If "we" use ASL and "they" use English, what happens to the "we" when we use English? Ambivalent feelings about self spring from such situations. The message is that it is not good to be too "hearing." There is a sign, "think hearing," used as a derogatory identification of such people; the concept is directly analogous to calling a black person an "Oreo."

What compounds these ambivalent feelings is that many Deaf people themselves do not recognize that ASL is a real language, having been carefully schooled by the dominant culture to think the contrary. Because Deaf people operate linguistically on a continuum between two languages, using many different varieties as the situation demands (Stokoe 1970:27; Markowicz and Woodward 1975:1-15), the possibility exists for greater ambivalence about their own language. Hence, anxiety can crop up when the Deaf attempt to define what they use. Often you will hear an informant say that he signs English or that ASL is really a simplified English. Bilingual play can serve as a mediating factor for the bilingual person who has to function between both languages, mediating the languages and the associated linguistic identity, which is often blurred. By looking at what "we" are and what "we" are not through a vehicle such as "Please b-u-t," a reaffirmation of what "Deaf" is occurs.

"To understand laughter," Bergson tell us, "we must put it back into its natural environment, which is society, and above all we must determine the utility of its function, which is a social one. Laughter," he continues, "must answer to certain requirements of life in common. It must have a social significa-tion (Bergson 1911:7). The joke is still told, is still laughed at, and still serves a purpose today for the simple fact that the con-flicts still exist. There are anxieties related to communication with the hearing world. There is ambiguity with reference to linguistic identity. The decision-makers in Deaf education are still predominantly hearing, still paternalistic. The programs for training teachers of the Deaf still, for the most part, either are based on oral methods, or focus on artificial sign systems based on English. Although improving, the majority culture remains largely uninformed.

Fry states that "a metaphor allows us to treat a psychologi-cal phenomenon as a concrete entity and allows us to gather together items of humor, wit, comedy, etc. into one circum-scribed object for contemplation" (1963:35). This joke is a metaphor for the language situation of the community, the ex-perience of the community within the hearing world and the search of the individual for identity. In each of these dimen-sions, the way is externally blocked. The language is dismissed; the culture is not recognized; and the individual is prevented from gaining true acceptance on any formal level within the hearing world. Thus, the joke reflects the very real conflict that exists between two cultures—hearing and Deaf—and at the same time serves as an aggressive outlet against the majority as well as a vehicle to reaffirm the group identity of the Deaf minority. "Please b-u-t" will continue to be an "old chestnut" as long as the indifference continues and the gates remain down.

10

What If...Alexander Graham Bell Had Gotten His Way?

Ben Bahan

IMAGINE YOURSELF watching a play: the scene is a dark alley, post-war America in the 1950's. There is a dim street light that beams down to a young couple who meet in secret. Susja, a young woman wearing ponytails and dark blue jeans with cuffs, is in her last year of school. Bruce, a mechanic who graduated from school a year ago, is wearing a T-shirt with rolled up sleeves, blue jeans and sneakers. They both have *ominous*-looking tattoos on their left arms imprinted with their "serial numbers."

SUSJA: I love you very much, but you know we can't marry. Do you want to leave this country? It's so difficult to do. My family is here; this is America, my country.

BRUCE: How can you want to live in this country so filled with hypocrisy—so famous for its "freedom," when we do not have any freedom at all? Look at these tattoos we have to wear just because we are deaf. By law, we can't marry. We are not free; America is a fascist nation!

Reproduced by permission of the author and *Deaf Community News*.

Susja and Bruce agonize over whether to defect to Canada or stay in America knowing they can never wed, despite the fact they are madly in love. In America all deaf people are branded with arm tattoos. Most have gotten them at residential schools for the deaf.

SUSJA: You know what will happen if we get caught, we are off to... (she cries).
BRUCE (comforting her): Yes I know, I know perfectly well, my uncle was sent there.
SUSJA: It's just like a concentration camp; no one survives the cold.

At that time, deaf people who defied the law were shipped off to labor camps in Alaska.
The play ends in a surreal dream. Cheap, dry ice - created fog flows all over the stage. The couple embraces surrounded by total darkness, but their togetherness, their bond, foretell a potentially happy ending.
Afterwards, you and your friends go out to Howard Johnson's for a drink and discuss the play. One friend shows you the program book. There is a message from the playwright on the back:
"This story is based on a would-be true *story* . It is based on information collected from many deaf people across America who were asked what they would do if they were prohibited from marrying. Most of them said they would defect. Many of them did not realize the events described in this play could have been *real*."

Defective 'Deaf Race'

In 1883, Alexander Graham Bell wrote an infamous paper for the National Science Academy entitled, "Memoirs Upon the Formation of the Deaf Variety of the Human Race." In this paper, Bell claimed a "defective deaf race" was emerging and growing strong. He argued this "defective race" was growing in size because deaf children were being "institutionalized." The result created intermarriages. Bell feared hearing society had created a "monster," in establishing residential schools for the deaf.

At that National Science Academy meeting in 1883, Bell gave a lengthy talk about the statistics of intermarriages. He argued that the frequent occurrence of deaf people with the last names of "Smith," "Brown," and "Miller" at the same school was proof that deaf people were marrying each other and having lots of deaf children.

But have you ever looked in the phone book and noticed how many "Smiths," "Browns," and "Millers" there are? Are they all related? Well, according to Bell, they were!

Bell believed that deaf people more than any single group tended to marry each other. In other words, he felt a deaf person was much more likely to marry another deaf person than, say a person with epilepsy was likely to marry another epileptic. Bell feared that somewhere along the line as generation after generation of deaf families intermarried, there would gradually come to be a pure deaf breed of people, or in other words: a *Deaf Race*.

Marriage for Deaf Prohibited

To me that's great! Imagine us being called a "race," instead of "handicapped." Yeah! Imagine saying to yourself: "I am a member of the Deaf Race."

However, one unfortunate aspect of Bell's view was he believed deafness was a plague which should be completely wiped off the face of the earth. He believed this so fiercely that he came up with two possible solutions. 1) *Preventative method:* Close all residential schools and place deaf kids in public schools with hearing kids. This would prevent many deaf couples from meeting in the first place, which might cause them to hold hands, which in turn might cause them to kiss, which might lead to marriage, etc. So, by preventing any possibility of deaf meeting deaf, Bell reasoned, there would be less chance of deaf people marrying each other. (Hearing society actually seems to be adopting this method today.) 2)*Repressive method:* Legally forbid deaf persons from marrying each other. Or, have Congress pass a law making it illegal for deaf people to marry at all. Yes, Bell went so far as to propose legislation forbidding the marriage of persons who came from families having more than one deaf member.

Those are the two solutions Bell suggested to solve the "deaf problem." I find it ridiculous on this account alone. Statistics tell us only 10% of deaf people have deaf parents, while 90% of deaf people have hearing parents. If this is true, then I would like to propose a *repressive method for hearing people:* Hearing people should never marry each other, because they create 90% of the deaf population!

Bell, in his worrisome thoughts, felt he had to solve the deaf problem to prevent the formation of a defective, diseased race. He came up with the two ideas mentioned above as a sort of "final solution." Did I say "final solution?" It seems eerie because Adolph Hitler used the same words in his quest to solve the "Jewish problem" during World War II. I am not saying their methods are similar, but the ideas are not that much different. Bell and Hitler both wanted to wipe out what they considered "defective."

There is a twist of irony to all this. There are some residential and day schools in this country that have portraits of this very man, Alexander Graham Bell, hanging on their walls. Yet in his paper, "Memoirs Upon the Formation of the Deaf Variety of the Human Race," this man criticized the whole idea of residential schools because he so badly wanted to eliminate deafness. Nevertheless, along these schools' hallowed halls there still hang portraits paying silent homage to Mr. Bell.

'Neo-Bell' Movement?

You may now sigh in relief that no one acted on his proposed solutions to the "deaf problem." but if you think about it, around 100 years after Bell, society has in some ways begun adopting his *preventative method* . Residential schools in America are facing hardships, and many more deaf kids are being mainstreamed with hearing kids than ever before. Deaf Clubs are facing membership enrollment problems because the core of the Deaf Community emerges from those residential schools.

So, you may say, "Well, A.G. Bell is history." I am warning you, history does repeat itself, if we do not learn from it. I predict there will be a "neo-Bell" movement in this country (Just like there is a Neo-Nazi movement alive in the world today.) When the movement comes it will be called "Neo-Bellism." But that's another story, another article. Besides, by then I'll probably have defected to Canada! I hear the air is clean up there.

11

Train-Gone-Sorry: The Etiquette of Social Conversations in American Sign Language

Stephanie Hall

DEAF AMERICANS using American Sign Language (ASL) often experience conflict with hearing Americans because of differing conventions of polite conversation. The ethnography of communication (Hymes 1964)) is used here to discover the conventions of politeness in a Deaf social club, where polite language is related to contrasting attitudes toward ASL and signing that imitates English syntax. Polite conversation is outlined in detail, including saying hello, turning one's back, ensuring comprehension, taking a person's hands, sharing information, and saying goodbye. The pattern of the conversations is examined to demonstrate how it differs from the conversational patterns of English speaking, hearing Americans. Conversations in ASL begin informally, get to the point quickly, then conclude formally and slowly. Conversely, conversations among hearing Americans are apt to begin formally and slowly and conclude informally and quickly. From these results two of the underlying social attitudes that give rise to the conventions of politeness in ASL are inferred: one should facilitate communication and one should promote unity among the Deaf.

Introduction.. Deaf persons using American Sign Language (ASL) in the United States, Canada, and some parts of the Caribbean consider themselves a cultural group and are remarkably close knit (Baker & Padden 1978). While many aspects of Western culture and language are common to them, their conventions of politeness often differ subtly from those of hearing people. Since these differences in conversational etiquette are rarely recognized, either by the Deaf or by the hearing people who associate with them, the conventions are often the source of friction in Deaf-hearing relations. [The term Deaf is used to denote members of this cultural group, since the term deaf commonly refers only to severe hearing loss.]

To discover these conventions of politeness, I have followed the example of Dell Hymes' ethnography of communication (Hymes 1964). Through participant observation in a Deaf social club in Southeastern Pennsylvania I was able to learn the rules for polite behavior, how these rules may be modified on appropriate occasions, what happens when a rule is broken, and most importantly, some underlying attitudes and assumptions prompting these rules of etiquette.

Because this ethnography was limited to one particular Deaf club, some of the examples may be found only in Southeastern Pennsylvania, or only in the socially relaxed setting of Deaf clubs. Like most areas in the United States with large populations of Deaf people, Southeastern Pennsylvania has regional dialects of ASL that must also be taken into account. Nevertheless, while some of the particular rules for interaction may be unique to this setting, I have made several generalizations that apply to all Deaf users of ASL and suggest directions for further ethnographic studies of this aspect of Deaf culture.

Signing that uses English word order or syntactic patterns has been given a variety of names; Manual English (Stokoe 1970), Ameslish (Bragg 1973), and Pidgin Sign English (Woodward 1972) among them. But as Woodward has pointed out, this variety of signing is not a discrete language but part of a continuum between ASL and English gesturally encoded

(Woodward 1980). In Southeastern Pennsylvania Deaf communities one must also consider "Mt. Airy Signs" (the dialect of Deaf people who attended the state school for the deaf in Mt. Airy, Philadelphia), as well as a Black sign language dialect brought to the state by Southern Black signers who migrated to the area, and the "college" or "modern sign language" used by Deaf Pennsylvanians who have attended Gallaudet College.

Nevertheless, as elsewhere in the United States, the most important distinction is between ASL and Anglicized signs. The latter are generally used in formal setting: church, lectures, school, and in the business meetings of the Deaf club. ASL is used in informal settings and in ordinary conversation. For the majority of Deaf Americans ASL is the first language in which they are truly fluent—whether they learn it in childhood or as adults. Thus they prefer to socialize in ASL, though most still feel that signing in English order is "better language."

Politeness in conversation at the Eastern Silent Club (a pseudonym) is influenced by these varieties of sign language and by its members' attitudes towards them. A speaker may choose English phrases with the words coded as manual signs, such as HOW ARE YOU, EXCUSE ME PLEASE, or ONE MINUTE PLEASE, or may select equivalent phrases from ASL, or use some variety between fully Anglicized signs and ASL. Even speakers who are not completely fluent in one language or the other usually know a number of stock phrases in both ASL and Anglicized signs, which they use in appropriate situations, trying to approximate the language in which the partner to the communication is more fluent. When Deaf people talk to the hearing, the hard-of-hearing, or the orally trained Deaf person who knows only a few signs, they often speak as they sign and sign in English word order. Except in these instances, the informal atmosphere of the club encourages the use of ASL, as it is the language of informality and familiarity.

Social status, age, and sex must also be considered when observing the conventions of verbal politeness. Deaf Pennsylvanians' attitudes toward gender roles are similar to those of other conservative Americans: women are responsible for home and family; men are expected to provide financial support and take care of dealings outside the home. At the Club, women are supposed to behave in a ladylike fashion as prescribed by the rules of the Ladies' Auxiliary. They are not allowed to gamble and may drink with extreme moderation, if at all. Younger people have more liberal attitudes about the roles of men and women, but even they are more conservative than their hearing peers. There is much deference to age by youth, and older Club members display a parental attitude toward younger people. This may not always be apparent to the hearing observer, as Deaf young people often enjoy joking relationships with their elders, but at critical times it is clear that the older people accept a parent role with the young. The officer and ex-officers of the Club are active in looking after young people and are especially deferred to by them. Similarly, classmates from a school for the deaf often behave like siblings and maintain close lifelong relationships. For many Deaf people, especially those whose hearing families may not use sign language, the Deaf community is their surrogate family.

Additional factors influencing a person's social status and behavior in the Deaf community arise from language ability and those things influencing it. Whether or not a person has Deaf parents, whether he was deafened before or after acquiring speech, and whether he is hard-of-hearing or deaf all may influence his mode of social interaction. Hard-of-hearing is a particularly difficult category to define, because a person can be physically hard-of-hearing (i.e. have enough hearing to understand amplified speech and use the telephone) and yet identify himself socially with the Deaf. Or the person may choose to identify himself as hard-of-hearing, a socially ambiguous status in both the hearing and the Deaf communities. The social importance given to the foregoing factors varies from individual to individual, depending on how the individual and his or her peers choose to call attention to them.

The following seven sections describe the conversational rules of etiquette I observed at the Eastern Silent Club. I have included as many variations or options for each circumstance as possible. To a certain extent the conventions I have noted are peculiar to the relaxed atmosphere of the Club. In all the cases I am describing the interactions of speakers known to each other; the etiquette of introductions and conversation with strangers is a vast topic in itself. Because most of the members of the Eastern Silent Club have known each other for many years, even a lifetime, the appearance of a stranger would be a special event. The interactions I describe are the more usual.

1. *Saying hello.* The special problems of deafness and of communicating in a visual language are unfamiliar to people who speak and hear. Getting the attention of a person to whom one would like to speak is no simple matter when that person cannot hear. If that person is not too far away it is customary to look him or her in the face until the look is returned, if not, to tap the person on the shoulder or upper arm. In the less than serious setting of the Club one can playfully jostle others to get their attention.

Physical contact is so commonly a part of Deaf communication that Deaf people find it amusing and sometimes puzzling when hearing people are startled or averse to being touched. Commonly, men touch other men, although when they embrace in greeting it is usually side by side rather than face to face. Older married men and women may touch or hug members of the opposite sex without restriction. Younger married people seem to express affection toward their friends of the opposite sex a little less freely, although they are certainly more relaxed in this regard than are hearing persons of the same age. Young unmarried friends who are not an established couple are more restrained in the manner in which they touch each other, hugging each other only side by side if at all. Since illicit flirting is difficult in a situation where everyone knows everyone else, married people are free to be physically affectionate with their friends and may even play at being flirtatious.

If the person one wants to converse with is too far away to touch, across the bar for example, getting attention is more difficult. A person may try waving to the friend in an exaggerated manner. If this does not work, the initiator may thump the bar or stamp on the floor, causing vibrations that the other may respond to: but this method is not favored because it often disturbs everyone in the vicinity. One can shout the name of the person called if he knows the other has enough hearing to respond. (This is the only instance in which voice communication is used unless hearing people are involved.) The person desiring another's attention may also try to get the attention of a third party closer to the person intended and get that one to attract the attention of the other.

These methods are also used to indicate to someone already engaged in conversation that one would like the next speaking turn. [Speaking turn is the technical term in ethnography of communication; here literally a signing turn is meant.] Another way to ask for a turn is to stand very close, touching or nearly touching shoulders.

The person engaged in a conversation acknowledges the presence and purpose of one who wishes to speak by taking his or her hand, by putting a hand on the other's shoulder or by signing "YES" or "ONE-FIVE" (lit. "just a minute"). The speaker (signer) can do one or other of these things but cannot look away from the person he or she is addressing if that one is signing; for this will disrupt the conversation. The person making a bid for a turn must also avoid disrupting the conversation in progress.

As often occurs, this rule became obvious to me only when it was broken. I was watching Mr. Q., the Club's former president and senior member, tell a story when Mrs. C. came up behind me and patted me on the arm. Startled, I turned to look at her (hearing habits die hard). Mr. Q. stopped in the middle of his narrative. "I thought you were telling a story," Mrs. C. signed.

Mr. Q. laughed and signed, "I was until you interrupted!"

"Sorry, go ahead. I'm paying attention," answered Mrs. C.

It is significant that from Mr. Q.'s perspective the interruption was caused by Mrs. C., not by me. Such interruptions are usually tolerated, unless an older person is interrupted by a younger person, as in this example. Although Mrs. C. has grown children, she is still Mr. Q.'s junior and, perhaps not insignificantly, a woman. Mr. Q.'s status in the Club gives him reason to expect that no one will interrupt him, although he is too good natured to get angry about it. Conversely, when young people are conversing and an older person wishes to speak to one of them, the younger people break off their conversation at once and never complain of being interrupted.

To greet another after getting attention, one may grasp a hand, hug the person, hold up a hand (the hand held still distinguishes this form of salute from the hand waved to get attention), or may fingerspell h-i. One may also sign "FINE?" or "HOW YOU?" [The question mark indicates that the manual sign represented by the gloss is accompanied by appropriate nonmanual behavior.] Younger people conversing with each other sometimes use the greeting "FEEL?" in the sense 'What's happening?'. To this the response is often "ZERO," 'Nothing's happening'—consciously or unconsciously parallel with the familiar Spanish-American routine: "Que pasa?" "Nada." Another appropriate response to FEEL? is "FINE FINE" to which the first responds "FINE FINE" to indicate that he also feels fine.

Names and name signs are not used when addressing someone except in formal situations and introductions. Usually names are used only to refer to someone absent.

2. *Taking turns.* Charlotte Baker-Shenk has noted several conventions of turn-taking by signers, such as holding for a moment the last sign made, looking into the face of the person one is speaking to, and/or putting one's hands to one's sides (Baker 1977). In special situations, there are additional turn-taking behaviors that can be used. Folding one's arms while frowning and leaning back a little is a device used to invite someone to take a turn or to insist that the other take a turn if reticent. This is often used as a way of demanding an opinion from someone. Rather than indicating disapproval [as the frown might suggest to a hearing person] the behavior conveys seriousness and insistence, although I do not think it would be appropriate for a younger person to address to someone older.

Baker-Shenk has also described two conventional "question faces." The first is an expression with eyebrows raised and head thrust forward. The second expression is one of eyebrows drawn together and chin raised. The first is used with yes-no questions and the second for wh- word questions (who, what, when, where, and why). The first expression used with a head-shake may be the response of the person questioned that one does not know the answer. The first expression is also used throughout the manual expression of a rhetorical question, even though such questions may begin with a wh- word (Baker 1980). To indicate that one wants the floor to ask a question one may make the first of these question faces and accompany it with a raised finger or the sign WAIT.

A shrug or open hands indicate one has nothing to say and gives the floor to someone else. Raised eyebrows with a smile or an open mouth ask for a turn when one has a sudden idea or inspiration. This facial signal may be emphasized with the manual sign KNOW, or in the case of an especially clever idea, the sign LIGHT made above the head. To request the floor while someone else is speaking in the case of a disagreement or misunderstanding one may hold up the index finger, or for a still more emphatic interruption, one may wave as when asking for attention.

3. *Ensuring comprehension.* During a lengthy speech a signer will often pause and ask his listeners "UNDERSTAND?" The speaker may be literally asking if everyone is following, or may be indicating that he has just made an important point and is providing an opportunity for the others to respond. This is particularly important when three or more people are participating in the conversation.

Ensuring comprehension in a language received visually requires that everyone involved in a conversation share responsibility for understanding. A speaker has several methods to make certain everyone is paying attention. If a participant is momentarily distracted the speaker will often pause until that one looks at him again. If a speaker becomes frustrated with a person who continues to be distracted, he will tap that one on the shoulder, wave, or if circumstances require an especially forceful expression, will sign "ATTENTION."

Listeners must keep their eyes directed toward the signer's face, but the signer may look away for a brief interval if the grammar of sign language demands it. The audience responds to the sign UNDERSTAND? with the manual signs YES,

RIGHT, or TRUE. In spite of these efforts, however, the speaker must sometimes repeat. An expression used to indicate frustration with having to repeat too often is the sign glossed TRAIN-GONE-SORRY, which translated means 'I am not going to repeat myself; you should have been paying attention the first time.' But I have never seen this used except in a joking manner when the speaker relented and repeated himself after all.

One is also expected to facilitate conversations other than those he is participating in. Politeness in this community requires one to move out of the way of people who are signing to each other and to convey an attention-requesting signal to someone who has not noticed it.

4. *Turning one's back.* As has already been emphasized, maintaining visual contact is essential in ASL. If one wishes to insult another all one need do is turn the head and close the eyes, thus cutting that person off. Done improperly, turning one's back on someone can also be interpreted as an insult.

When circumstances make it necessary for someone in a conversation to turn away, he can sign ONE-FIVE 'just a minute' and explain what he is about to do. He can also maintain physical contact with his conversational partner by putting a hand on that one's shoulder or arm or knee if sitting. Two unusual methods of turning around occurred at the Club. One that seems to be used by older women with each other is to take the hand of the person one is conversing with and then turn around and sign briefly to another. The other, used by older men when they must turn their backs on a lady, is for the man to take the lady's hand under his elbow while speaking to someone else. This latter resembles formal etiquette among hearing people. Both of these forms struck me as unusual, because it is generally impolite to take the hand of another person except to shake hands. Inquiring among Deaf people in other areas and among younger people in Southeastern Pennsylvania, I found that they also regarded as strange, even unacceptable, these ways of capturing a hand when one must turn away during a conversation.

The etiquette of turning around is rarely violated except in anger, although other strong emotions are sometimes an excuse for turning improperly. I once observed a widow complaining to friends that she was lonely and missed her husband. They responded that she should get out and do things more; their husbands were often off at work or playing cards with friends but they did not feel lonely. Turning away from the group, the widow signed, "You don't understand" and walked off. The other women shook their heads at each other, and then one of them went over and took the widow by the shoulders, said something to her which made her laugh, and brought her back to the group. No one was angry, nor did the woman seem terribly upset. Apparently her grief and her need to communicate something beyond words excused what would otherwise have been unacceptable behavior.

5. *Taking another's hands.* Although it is usually acceptable to take another person's hand in greeting or to touch the hands of a person who is not signing, it is extremely rude to take another person's hands to stop them from signing. As Baker-Shenk has observed, this is the equivalent of putting a hand over the mouth of a person speaking (Baker 1980). I have seen this rule violated only once, by no less a person than the president of the Club. He was trying to get the attention of a woman who was very angry with him. She was signing violently and ignored his emphatic waving. Finally he stopped her hands with his, then signed, 'Please, I'm sorry; please, you misunderstand me.' He then proceeded to explain himself. I believe that few people of lesser social standing could have got away with this no matter how much they apologized. His action was parental and therefore allowed because as Club president he holds the status of a parent.

6. *Sharing information.* Members of the Club do not attempt to hold private conversations, for generally privacy is difficult in sign language. Once a conversation is begun, anyone who wishes to may join in or watch. Conversations between only two people do not last long before they are joined by others. Privacy can be had by signing very small, by fingerspelling behind a hand, or by going behind closed doors. But secrecy, except as a joke, is not considered appropriate in the social setting of the Club and so may be considered rude. If one receives

a call on the Club's TTY, one must expect to share its contents with friends afterwards.

Hearing people often comment that Deaf people do not keep secrets among themselves—although they may keep their secrets from hearing people! Yet it should not be surprising that among people for whom all information is precious, even sacred, secrecy is considered anti-social. Sharing information is an affirmation of the unity of the Deaf community. Deaf people in turn often think a hearing person's attitude toward privacy infuriating and perplexing.

7. *Saying Good-bye.* Leavetaking in this community is always fairly formal and lengthy. When a person finishes a conversation, he must explain where he is going and what he is going to do. The other person will then reciprocate. Conversations are never considered completely over until everyone leaves for the night, at which time people look for their friends to say good night to them. As might be expected, this process can take a long time. People put on their coats and head slowly for the door, finally leaving as much as an hour or two later. As they say good night to each other they sign expressions like: GOOD-NIGHT, IT WAS GOOD TO SEE YOU, I WILL SEE YOU NEXT WEEK, I'M HAPPY YOU CAME TONIGHT, and so on. These phrases may be accompanied by a hug and a kiss or squeezing hands. People almost always indicate when they will see each other again, sometimes repeating the date and the place several times. Since the opportunities for face-to-face interaction among Deaf friends in their native language are limited and treasured, leaving the Club is a sad affair. Leaving too quickly might also deny someone the opportunity to talk to one; so indicating repeatedly that one is about to leave is a way of announcing to friends that if they want to say something they had better do so.

Conversational pattern. Considering the pattern of conversations as wholes, it is interesting that interactions often begin informally and jokingly and end formally and seriously. People say 'hello' in ASL; they often say "good-bye' in more formal Anglicized signs. The pace of conversation is rapid at the beginning—people say hello and get straight to the point—but ending the conversation is a gradual process. Getting to the point and being direct is never rude, as it sometimes is in hearing conversations; while ending abruptly as is sometimes done in American English interchanges, may be construed to mean that the person so ending the conversation does not care about the other. This could be one source of hearing people's complaints that Deaf people are too blunt (at beginning); likewise of Deaf people's feeling that hearing people do not care about them or talk down to them.

While it is easy to see why partings from friends who make up an extended family might be lengthy, it is less easy to explain why these partings must contain the formality of phrases signed in English word order. I have noticed that peers may sometimes part informally by patting one another on the shoulder and waving, but non-peers nearly always use phrases signed in English phraseology. Perhaps the special familial relationships between the old and the young are reaffirmed by a formal parting.

People often make a point of saying good night to the president of the Club, particularly the revered former president, Mr. Q. As young people leave they are often told to be careful and to be good. Young women are cautioned not to go to their cars alone. Although I suspect that the young people sometimes get tired of having so many parents, they seem to take this parting advice with respect and make an effort to say good night to certain older people as they leave.

Once when Mr. Q. was leaving for the night, a young man came up behind him and poked him in the ribs. "Why are you leaving so soon? The night is young!" he asked. "Oh, I'm a busy man. I have to get up early," answered Mr. Q. (This was a joke; at eighty-three, Mr. Q. has earned his retirement.) The two continued to joke for a moment, then the young man signed to me: "You know, Mr. Q. is a very important man here at the Eastern Silent Club. He has watched many, many Deaf people grow up. Many Deaf people look up to him." Mr. Q. Stood up to demonstrate his five-foot-two stature. "They don't have to look up very far!" he cracked. Then as he began a round of good nights, he paused and asked the young man and me, "Will I see you next Wednesday?" We replied he would, "Now you be a good girl," he signed to me.

In this exchange the young man broke off his joking manner to make a formal declaration of respect. Mr. Q. reestablished the joking relationship with his quip, then reasserted his parental role with his admonitions as he left the Club. In this particular instance the young man's speech about Mr. Q. was certainly an exaggerated display of respect for my sake (perhaps in case I misinterpreted their joking), but it demonstrates the reaffirming of relationships that may occur as people leave the Club.

Perhaps as the Deaf Club members go out into the relatively hostile hearing world they feel the need to reassure themselves that they have a home and a family that will be there when they return. The formality of Anglicized signs aids in this small ritual of saying good night, in effect, to all of the Deaf community.

Conclusion.—One basic principle of etiquette seems to be clear despite its complex manifestations: one should always act in a way that facilitates communication and access to information. Rudeness inhibits communication—whether it is by keeping a secret, turning one's back on someone improperly, or leaving the Club too hastily. This basic rule also explains why some behavior that is rude among hearing people, blunt speech or telling a secret, is not rude among the Deaf.

Another underlying principle of verbal politeness suggests that people must act in a way that will promote unity among the Deaf. To act well one is expected to share everything from personal experiences and the content of TTY messages to one's poker and raffle winnings. Open displays of affection such as hugging, kissing, and jostling solidify ties and demonstrate one's positive attitude to everyone nearby. This feeling, that unity must be actively promoted, also fosters the sense of obligation Deaf Club members feel toward one another. Maintaining unity is related to the principle of facilitating communication because sharing information and keeping the lines of communication open are also ways of promoting group unity.

Hearing people, even those who work closely with the Deaf, rarely perceive fully the culture of the Deaf community. Those who do come to understand some aspects of that culture, such as these rules of conversational etiquette, must do so by trial and error. Often they fail to understand cultural differences between Deaf and hearing communities—differences that may begin with the very way in which Deaf people and hearing people say hello to one another.

12

The Deaf Child as a Linguistic Minority

Veda R. Charrow
Ronnie B. Wilbur

THE PROBLEM of educating deaf children can be looked at from two points of view. Traditionally, deaf children have been regarded as a handicapped group, whose inability to hear imposed severe limitations on how they could learn. It cannot be denied that deaf children, compared to hearing children, are in fact handicapped: they lack the ability to hear spoken language.

But there is another way of viewing deaf children: as a linguistic minority, like Mexican–Americans, or Chinese–Americans, or other non-native English speakers. Prelingually deaf children, after all, are not really aware of this "handicap," since they do not know what "normal hearing" is. It is only when they were required to look, perform, behave and achieve like hearing children that they begin to see themselves as "not normal"—as opposed to merely deaf. For all intents and purposes, however, a deaf child with no other handicaps is "normal," and very comparable in many ways to a minority child whose native language is not English. The catch is that the deaf child's normal modality for language is not auditory and oral, but visual and manual.

This may appear to be a strange way of characterizing the "handicap" of prelingual deafness, but the analogy between deafness and minority cultures holds in more ways than one. First, most prelingually deaf persons do not learn an auditory-vocal language as their native language. Prelingually deaf American children learn English in school, laboriously, as though it were a foreign language (Charrow and Fletcher, 1974), and the English they end up with is usually not the grammatical standard English that we know (Charrow, 1975a; Wilbur and Quigley, 1975). Second, most prelingually deaf persons do have a native language, and that is American Sign Language—ASL (or "Ameslan"; Fant, 1972). Nearly 500,000 deaf people use ASL, making it the third most widely used non-English language in the United States (Spanish, 4 1/2 million, Italian, 631,000). It is estimated that when hearing people who have learned ASL are included, the total number of users is double or triple this figure (O'Rourke, Medina, Thames and Sullivan, 1975). This is in spite of the fact that ASL is not taught in any schools, and its use by teachers and students has been prohibited in many schools (Alterman, 1970). Third, there is a deaf community—a deaf culture—whose rules for social interaction, behavioral standards, politeness conventions, and even amusements, are not the same as those of the dominant—hearing—culture. The main difference between the deaf community, and let us say, the Chicano community, is that only 10 percent of its members are born into it, as deaf children of deaf parents. The other 90 percent become members by learning ASL and by being accepted into the deaf community.

All of these factors—the fact that most deaf children do not learn English as a true native language; their ability to learn ASL as a native language; and the existence of a deaf community, to which most prelingually (and many postlingually) deaf youngsters and adults belong—have an important bearing on the education and language development of deaf children in North America. We will discuss each of these factors in relation to deaf education. We will emphasize, particularly, the concept of deaf children as a linguistic minority, whose linguistic and cultural rights should be respected, rather than the older view of deaf children as flawed and somehow incomplete children, who must be made to look and act like hearing children.

We will first provide some background into the intellectual capabilities and general educational achievement of prelingually deaf people in America, and then discuss the English competence of deaf children.

Intellectual Abilities

Traditionally, deaf persons were thought to be inferior to the hearing population in cognitive abilities (Bereiter and Engelmann,1966). More recently, however, numerous studies have indicated that prelingually deaf persons are comparable to the hearing population in their range and distribution of intelligence (Mindel and Vernon, 1971), and ability to conceptualize and reason (Furth, 1971). Deaf persons had been thought to be intellectually and cognitively inferior for what seemed to be common-sense reasons. It was thought that (1) most prelingually deaf persons had no language, (2) language was necessary for thought, and therefore (3) most prelingually deaf persons had a "cognitive deficit"—an inability to think, conceptualize, and reason. However, there are a number of fallacies underlying this chain of reasoning.

First and most important, there is a general confusion of "language" with speech. Because people who are born deaf—or who have become deaf before age two—cannot hear speech, and have difficulty learning spoken language, they were thought to have no language at all. But language is not necessarily speech, as we shall demonstrate in our discussion of sign language; nor is speech necessarily language, as anyone who is acquainted with a parrot knows.

Second, there is the confusion between language and English. This is a confusion which has been observed in areas other than deafness. (Picture, if you will, the nineteenth colonial Englishman, or the "ugly American" tourist, in India or Africa, who refuses to learn the "outlandish gibberish" of those "foreign **natives**" because it is not really language, just grunts—and anyway, **why** can't the natives learn a real language, like English?). **Languages** differ; English is not the only real language in the world. Languages which are not structured in the same way as English are not deficient, or "non-language." We cannot use English as a basis for judging the "grammaticalness" or validity of any other language.

Thus, deaf persons whose speech is poor, or who know little or no English, are not necessarily "language deficient." If they have a language such as ASL (and most prelingually deaf adolescents and adults do)—even if it does not look like English or other Indo-European languages—then they are not languageless. The investigators who used deaf subjects as "languageless" controls in studies of cognitive ability did not, in general, take knowledge of ASL into account, and thereby confounded their experiments. Those who were more careful, and used young deaf subjects, whose competence in ASL was still minimal, demonstrated that the thinking and reasoning processes of deaf children are still very similar to those of hearing children (Furth, 1971; Furth and Youniss, 1971; Youniss, Furth and Ross, 1971).

Educational Achievement

Despite the similarity in the intelligence and the cognitive abilities of deaf and hearing persons, the educational attainment of deaf children is far below that of hearing children with similar backgrounds. This is understandable, since prelingually deaf children usually have great difficulty learning English. As almost all education depends on a knowledge of English, this is indeed an unfortunate situation. At this point one might ask, "Why don't deaf children know English? Aren't they taught it in school? Why hasn't someone found better ways of teaching them English?" The problem is not at all simple.

Indeed, deaf children are taught English in school. They are taught it for as many years as they are in school; many take courses in remedial English after high school, as well. In many schools, deaf children are taught English orally, through lipreading, speech lessons and auditory amplification. This method—"oralism"—has not been successful in teaching English to the majority of prelingually deaf children, for a number of reasons. For one thing, it takes a certain talent to lipread adequately. There is no proof that deaf children are any more talented at lipreading than hearing children. Furthermore, even the best lipreaders can only "read" about 40 percent of what a speaker is saying; they fill in the rest from their experience and their knowledge of English, if they can. Second, it is impossible to lipread (or "speechread") English without first knowing the structure (to determine, for example the probability that a given word will precede or follow another word. Try lipreading a Russian film, knowing only a few Russian words and no Russian grammar). Third, it is impossible to learn English from lipreading alone. There is no indication of word boundaries, certain sound units (phonemes) are invisible, others are indistinguishable from each other (/b/ and /p/, for example); in general, too much information is lost. If this looks like a vicious circle, it probably is, and it helps to explain the many "errors" and non-standard constructions in English that graduates of our finest schools for the deaf make (cf. Charrow, 1975a; Quigley, Smith and Wilbur, 1974).

In some other schools, English is taught—along with all other subjects—by means of the oral method plus fingerspelling; this is sometimes called the Rochester Method. Words and sentences are spelled out, letter by letter, using the (one-handed) manual alphabet, simultaneously with the spoken word or sentence (Scouten, 1967). This method probably helps somewhat, as it provides more visual input, but it is still heavily dependant on prior knowledge of English, besides being slow and tiring, and thus cannot be considered an ideal instructional medium. (To give yourself an idea of what the Rochester Method is like, have someone read you the previous paragraph letter-by-letter).

In a growing number of schools, various forms of Signed English and Manual English are used along with speech and speechreading in programs of "Total Communication." We are using the term Signed English to refer to the use of ASL signs in

English word-order, with occasional fingerspelling for those items that have no traditional ASL equivalents (e.g., "the," "of"). The term Manual English is used for specially-devised sign systems such as Seeing Essential English, or SEE I (Anthony, 1971), Signing Exact English, or SEE II (Gustason, Pfetzing, Zawolkow and Norris, 1972), Systematic Sign Language, or the Paget Gorman Sign System (Paget and Gorman, 1969), Linguistics of Visual English, or LOVE (Wampler, 1971), and Manual English (Washington State School for the Deaf, 1972). Such systems often invent their own signs, and attempt to duplicate in signs the entire morphology—word-formation system—of English (e.g., there are signs for "-ing," "-ed," "-tion," "-ance/-ence," "a-," "un-," "de-," etc.). Manual English systems (as opposed to Signed English) were devised on the (as yet untested) assumption that because they look like English, they will enable the deaf child to learn English in a more natural manner. (See Charrow, 1975b: Wilbur, 1976, in press: for a discussion of the potential problems involved.)

Studies have shown that prelingually deaf children with early manual communication—ASL or some variety of Signed English—do consistently better in all school subjects, including English, than comparable deaf children with only oral communication (Vernon and Koh, 1970: Mindel and Vernon, 1971; Brasel and Quigley, 1975).

Nonetheless, the general educational achievement of even those deaf students who are fluent in a manual language is well below that of comparable hearing students (Moores, 1970; Marshall and Quigley, 1970). The situation is similar to that of other minority children who are not educated in their native language.

English Competence

Studies of the English language skills of prelingually deaf students have shown many errors—often called "deafisms"—present in their English productions, both oral and written (cf. Quigley, Smith and Wilbur, 1974; Wilbur and Quigley, 1975). We have suggested (Charrow, 1975a; Wilbur, 1976) that such errors are not random, but are rule-governed; they might be considered "variable rules," co-existing with English rules. Such rules appear to be based upon incorrect hypotheses about the structure of English, which deaf children cannot immediately correct because of their limited exposure to, and feedback from, English. Wilbur, Quigley and Montanelli (1975) found that at least one deviant rule decreased significantly with age. In general, however, few prelingually deaf children end up with full competence in Standard English.

In order to test the hypothesis that prelingually deaf children were learning English as though it were a foreign language, Charrow and Fletcher (1974) gave the Test of English as a Foreign Language (TOEFL) to deaf high-school students of college-entrance age. Although the deaf subjects did not perform as well as foreign college entrants, in general their results more closely resembled those of foreign students than those of native speakers of English.

American Sign Language

There is only one language that prelingually deaf children in America can and do learn as a native language—without formal instruction, in a relatively short time—and that is American Sign Language.

ASL is not a universal sign language, as is sometimes thought, nor is it related to the sign language of the Plains Indians. ASL is historically related to French Sign Language (as it was originally brought here from France in the early 19th century by Laurent Clerc), but the two are no longer mutually intelligible (cf. French and Spanish, which are related, but are no longer mutually intelligible).

Until recently, ASL was considered by many educators of the deaf, and by many deaf people themselves, to be "ungrammatical" or even "lacking a grammar." It was also thought to be either very "concrete" (like pointing), or very "conceptual" (raw concepts thrown together, without any syntax); this is contradictory, to say the least. This was because ASL was looked at from the point of view of the structure of English.

No language can be judged relative to other languages: syntactic structures which a language appears to "lack" are invariably compensated for in some other way. Furthermore, any language, translated word-for-word, into English, looks strange, outlandish and ungrammatical. And yet, traditional observations of ASL do just that: translate ASL sentences, sign-for-word into English, overlooking many features which are crucial to the grammers of sign languages (such meaning-bearing features as directionality, facial expressions, and others).

Within the last fifteen years, however, linguists have begun to study ASL, and have found it to be a true language, with a complex grammatical structure, capable of expressing anything within human experience and imagination. It is also very different from English. (See Bonvillian, Charrow and Nelson, 1973; and Wilbur, 1976, for a comparison of some of the grammatical features of English and ASL.) ASL has grammatical structures undreamed of in English and other spoken languages: it uses the direction of the verb to indicate Agent-Verb-Object and other such relations, and can, in certain circumstances, express two ideas simultaneously—one with each hand. In addition, ASL inflects certain nouns for time (as "one week ago," "two years hence," in which the number and the past or future indicator are incorporated into the sign for "week" and "year"), and inflects various verbs for habitualness, iteration and certain semantic relationships by means of reduplication (repeating the sign), horizontally sweeping the arm, or rocking the body while signing (Fischer and Gough, 1979). There are many other grammatical mechanisms in ASL which have been described by linguists; still others are under investigation.

Studies of both deaf and hearing children of deaf parents have shown that ASL is acquired spontaneously, as a first language, in much the same way that a spoken language is acquired (Bellugi and Klima, 1972: Wilbur and Jones, 1974). Hearing and hard-of-hearing children of deaf parents usually learn ASL and English at the same time, in the same way that hearing bilinguals learn their two languages (Wilbur and Jones, 1974).

Nonetheless, as we mentioned previously, ASL is not used as a medium of instruction in schools for the deaf (except by a very few teachers, unofficially, when they find that students do not understand the spoken word, or the Signed or Manual English). Indeed, relatively few teachers of the deaf know ASL, and those who do are often hampered by their own attitudinal biases against it—as well as by educational policies that prohibit its use. Such biases and policies have thus far prevented the use of ASL as a medium of instruction in schools for the deaf.

The Deaf Community

In recent years, sociolinguists have begun to study linguistic/cultural minorities in America. With the increase in knowledge about "language communities," there has arisen a greater awareness of the diversity of languages and cultures in America, and the problems faced by linguistic/cultural minorities in the "melting pot." The melting pot aim—to "Americanize" minorities—may be admirable from one point of view (after all, one way to eliminate discrimination is to eliminate any differences). In practice,however, this aim is impractical—if not impossible—as well as damaging to the minority cultures involved. "Americanization" has meant loss of identity and cultural pride, rejection of cultural values and the disappearance of entire language groups in the United States. (Indeed, if ASL were not the only possible means of communication for the majority of deaf Americans, it too would probably have been wiped out long ago.) When linguists, psychologists, sociologists, and educators began to understand these problems, bilingual education programs began to be established, and emphasis began to be placed on cultural pride—on the diversity of the U.S. population, rather than its uniformity. This was true not only for immigrants, but also for black people and native Americans. "Black English," which had been considered "erroneous usage," or "ungrammatical English," gained respectability as a dialect of English (Baratz, 1969), and the concept of "language communities" whose cultures were different from the mainstream American Protestant culture became accepted.

About that time, linguists became interested in ASL (Stokoe, 1960,1971; McCall, 1965). In their investigations of ASL, they found that deaf signers (the majority of prelingually deaf persons and of those who became deaf in their youth) constitute not merely a linguistic minority, but also a language community (Schein, 1968; Padden, Markowicz, 1975). Although there are individual deaf communities in various parts of the U.S. and Canada (often near some institution or facility for the deaf, such as Gallaudet College), we can refer to an American "deaf community." This is because all the individuals in each deaf community share the same language—ASL—as well as their common "handicap" of deafness, and similar experiences in various institutions for the deaf and in the outside world. (It should be noted, however, that black southern signs are often different from ASL signs, a result of segregation; J. Woodward, personal communication.) It is ASL, above all else, which truly defines the deaf community. Native signers (deaf children of deaf parents) are automatically members of the deaf community, but such persons account for only 10 percent of the prelingually deaf persons in America. Deaf children of hearing parents become members of the deaf community by learning ASL from their peers who know it (although use of ASL may be prohibited in a school, a child who knows it is accorded high status, and it is likely that other students will learn ASL from him or her). Since very few deaf people can ever become truly "accepted" members of the hearing world, and because ASL is the only language that most deaf Americans learn spontaneously and use fluently, it is only natural that its users should be drawn together by it, into a language community.

Sociolinguistic studies of ASL and the deaf community have shown that there are different social conventions and politeness rules for signers than for speakers/listeners. Baker (1975) has described turn-taking in ASL conversation, and has shown that there are different "signals" for turn-taking in ASL than in English. There are, as well, different conventions regarding eye-contact, and distance between signer and addressee, than among hearing persons in the dominant culture. These and other such rules create some real "cultural" differences between the deaf and hearing communities.

The existence of a deaf culture is evident, too, in the various deaf theater and mime groups in this country (probably the best-known group is the National Theater of the Deaf, in the U.S.). There is also great interest in dance, and in "signed songs," on the stage, and occasionally on television.

Thus, despite what hearing people regard as the "handicap" of deafness, and despite the real problems that deaf children face in learning English and achieving, scholastically, deaf people who have been allowed to become fluent in ASL are not to be regarded as a collection of isolated unfortunates. They are a linguistic and cultural minority, with the security of a community, and rights which should be respected.

Recommendations and Conclusions

Our focus in this paper has been upon the deaf as an ASL-using community, out of the English-using mainstream. We believe that this focus is necessary, in order to develop reasonable, realistic solutions to the educational problems of prelingually deaf children. Most deaf persons, including deaf children, are not—and realistically cannot be—fully participating and benefiting members of the hearing community. There is no way at present to make deaf people hear. Deaf children should thus be accepted for what they are—deaf—and what they realistically can become: productive members of a linguistic/cultural minority group, with as much contact as possible with the hearing society. Only when there is such acceptance can educators begin to tackle the real problems of deaf children in a hearing society.

We have discussed the fact that American Sign Language is the only true native language of deaf children of deaf parents in America, and the only true first language of most deaf children of hearing parents. The use of Total Communication—with Signed or Manual English—is a partial concession to this fact. Educators of the deaf have recently been more willing to admit that it is much easier for prelingually deaf children to learn and use a manual/visual language than an auditory/vocal one. However, deaf students may not in fact be using the Signed or Manual English that their teachers are using. Deaf children use ASL among themselves, and it appears that they modify Signed or Manual English when they learn it, to make it conform more to the ASL they know (William Stokoe, personal communication; [Ed: see also Supalla, in press]). It is normal that they do this, since Signed English and the various Manual Englishes are inventions—with no native speakers—which can be used successfully only when one already knows English. Nonetheless, the fiction is maintained that the children fully understand the Signed or Manual English of their teachers, and learn correct English from it.

It might be more realistic, and successful, if procedures similar to the ones used in bilingual education programs for minority children were followed in teaching English to deaf children. Ideally, in the earliest years, deaf children should learn ASL. Once ASL is established as a means of communication, teachers can then use it as a medium of instruction for all subjects, including English—which can be taught along with speech, speech-reading and reading.

Such a program would require that more teachers be fluent in ASL, which would in turn require that biases against ASL be discarded. A first step, then, would be to train more teachers of the deaf to use ASL and understand its structure, and to improve the attitudes of all persons—deaf and hearing, teacher and student—toward ASL.

In the meantime, efforts to use any manual/visual language should be encouraged. ASL-users and Signed English-users have been found to perform significantly better than orally-trained students on tests of English and general achievement (Brasel and Quigley, 1975). They had obviously received more and earlier language input and practice than the orally-trained children. The educator of the deaf should nonetheless bear in mind that the Signed and Manual English systems described above may not in fact be teaching "straight English" to the children, and he or she should not have overly high expectations of it (Charrow, 1975b; Wilbur, 1976).

As long as deaf children are thought of as "flawed" hearing children, who should be learning English, but who somehow cannot learn it properly, their chances of learning Standard English and achieving in school are poor. But once deaf children are considered in the same light as other non-English-speaking minority children, with their own language, culture and social conventions, their educational lot and their relations with the hearing world are bound to improve.

13

Total Communication: A Total Farce

Ben Bahan

"WE WANT T.C. We want T.C.!" one elderly man signed as he walked with a group of deaf people carrying placards in a picket line before the New Jersey state house in Trenton.

I remember the movement vividly as a teenager; the deaf community was finally involved in educational concerns of deaf youth. They did that because many of them had suffered from ineffective educational methods used in schools across the country that forced them to use a mode they were not capable of mastering.

As a young man I was deeply moved by the idea we deaf people can do something about our lives and our children's educational upbringing. As a result of the movement, more schools adopted the total communication (TC) philosophy. Back then it seemed like a dream finally reached. A dream that was once considered impossible was made possible.

TC Revisited

Let's analyze what TC really means: it's a philosophy of teaching, not a method, that states teachers should use whatever method deemed appropriate (believed to be right) for the

---

Reproduced by permission of the author and *Deaf Community News*.

child. If the child would benefit from being taught orally, then oral methods should be adopted: if the child would benefit more from a manual method (sign language) in the classroom, then a manual method should be used, the philosophy states.

Over ten years have passed since the TC movement came to rest. Now it looks like TC is the most misinterpreted philosophy of all time.

Go to schools today and you'll find that TC usually means talking and signing at the same time (simultaneous communication). The philosophy of TC allows us to employ the simultaneous method, but we must realize that the simultaneous method is not TC.

TC's a Compromise

TC has turned into an educational compromise, a merge between two extreme methodologies: oralism and manualism. Whereas TC as a philosophy allows us to utilize one method alone within the framework of the needs of a given child, today it is made into a compromise where all children receive the same treatment. For that reason alone total communication has turned into a total farce.

In an attempt to unify the two methods (oral and manual) the education system created a diversity that confuses children. After schools finally accepted TC, educators began to realize they needed to develop a sign language system to match English word-for-word.

They set out to develop manually coded English systems; at one point in the past ten years there were several systems across the country: SEE 1, SEE 2, LOVE (Linguistics Of Visual English), and several other systems created by the state schools. The same thing occurs for oral approaches: more teachers are being forced to instruct speech without sufficient training and the emergence of cued speech has crept into the school systems along with the adopting of TC.

I'm not saying we should abandon TC, which has good intentions. It is the way the education system interprets this philosophy that we should abandon.

An Ineffective Approach

Too many schools use the simultaneous method of communication, which is ineffective. Research studies back the notion that teachers are not good language models when they sign and talk at the same time. The problem is either, 1) teachers would be talking more than signing, and when they do that the kids get less visual input, and the input they get visually is usually ungrammatical because the grammatical aspects are already spoken for, but not signed, or 2) teachers would sign more than they talk, which has the opposite problems from the first approach.

Either way, the kids suffer from poor linguistic models when the schools use their own version of TC which is really the simultaneous method.

Totalled Communication

One problem with the philosophy is its reliance on whatever method fits the child best. If we go to one classroom, we may have seven kids, each one with different needs.

How will the teacher meet the needs of each child? It places an unnecessary burden on the teachers, to have them use seven different methods to teach a subject. It's also time-consuming on the children, too.

Imagine a teacher going over this sentence: George Washington never chopped down a cherry tree. Seven times for each child's need, using oral method, Rochester Method (fingerspelling all the words in the sentence), SEE 2, writing, simultaneous method, drawing, and, if necessary for a child, Morse code.

When the teacher finally finishes her sentence seven different times, it might be time for the child to go to another class.

Instead of "total communication" happening in that classroom, all communication gets totalled.

A Better Way

The TC philosophy allows us to include one method/approach that has not been used in deaf education in our lifetime, and perhaps not in your parents' lifetime. That method would be the best thing that could happen for deaf children today: bilingualism.

Schools across the nation may know that deaf children use ASL as their preferred language, but they tend to refuse to use it in the classroom. With an open atmosphere of learning two languages at the same time in a classroom, it wouldn't be surprising to find the kids learning English faster and better.

We still have some questions to tackle before we can have an effective bilingual program; for example, how do we use English?

I would not use SEE. A good way to introduce English would be the way English is used: orally with a visual reinforcer, probably fingerspelling, when you "talk" to the students in an English classroom. However, the best way to introduce English would be none other than reading and writing. In a healthy, bilingual environment the kids would benefit tremendously, since they would learn two languages. Once we get the bilingual approach situation ironed out we would have a true TC environment.

The potential results are exciting. No matter what language you prefer.

14

A Bilingual, Bicultural Approach to Teaching English (How Two Hearies and a Deafie Got Together to Teach English)

Tom Humphries

Bette Martin

Terry Coye

THIS PAPER discusses a bilingual, bicultural approach to teaching English. Changing attitudes about languages and language learning and resolving cultural conflicts between the deaf and hearing cultures is the most important focus of the

Reproduced by permission of the National Association of the Deaf from F. Caccamise and D. Hicks (eds.), American Sign Language in a Bilingual, Bicultural Context. Proceedings of the Second National Symposium on Sign Language Research and Teaching.

approach. Discussion is limited to affective objectives because it is felt that the affect is the strongest and most important influence on language learning. Team-teaching is emphasized as a way to bring hearing and deaf, ASL and English users into the same classroom and model cross-cultural behavior. Some methods and materials for using ASL to teach English are described and demonstrated. Some results and reactions of students are given and the authors' feelings about the approach are discussed.

Introduction

In this paper, we write from experience and from our own learning and observations over many years of teaching English to young deaf adults. We write from the background of having tried many of the current techniques and materials for teaching English to deaf students. We write with a definition of ourselves as English language teachers rather than "language" teachers, a difference which is important in the sensitive world of English/ASL, deaf/hearing that we live in. The use of "language development" rather than "English language development" with deaf people has often implied that deaf people had *no* language, that ASL was not a real language, and that any form other than standard English had no utility. It was assumed that standard English was *the* language.

English is the first language of each of us (Tom, Bette, and Terry), and we are very aware of the need for it in this English-speaking society. However, we do not agree that one language is better than another. We face the fact that ASL is the native language of many deaf people and that it is as important to them as English is to us and other native users of English. We hope that our teaching reflects our belief that there are two

No implication should be drawn from the order in which the authors are listed. Our contributions to this paper, like our contributions to the ideas it describes, were equal. Tom Humphries is Associate Dean with the San Diego Community College District; Bette Martin is Special Assistant to the President of Gallaudet University; Terry Coye is Associate Professor of English at Gallaudet University.

complete and valuable languages that must co-exist with each other and receive equal respect and attention, and our acceptance of two cultures, the hearing culture and the deaf culture.

We believe that ASL can and does have, for many deaf people, the same function English has for English speakers: the capacity to transmit a culture, a way of life, and happiness. We know that English can add to this happiness just as ASL added to our happiness when we began to learn it. We do not believe that English is crucial to the happiness of all deaf people nor that as English teachers we are the bearers of happiness. At best, we are only the bearers of certain knowledge about English and some techniques for learning it.

We have spent much time in our classes talking about language attitudes, about language variation, about English and about ASL. We have spent much time talking about the differences between the deaf and hearing cultures. Why do we do this? Because we want to learn. Our students have as much to teach us as we them. We hope that our students know that we take as much as we give and that they are giving as they take from us. If this happens in our classroom, we are delighted. We want a bilingual, bicultural classroom in which differences are not just accepted, but valued, because we think that is the best learning situation. If we can talk openly, deaf and hearing people, in a classroom, as anywhere, we can be co-learners. We have profited from our experience in that we have become more bicultural and bilingual ourselves in a world where few people are lucky enough to be so. And we have had the pleasure of watching our students share that experience.

The Problem

Why hadn't our students learned English before coming to us? We felt it was not from lack of appropriate materials. There are a lot of materials for specific purposes that have been refined to the point that it would be hard to improve on them. We felt it was not from lack of appropriate teaching. There are many good teachers around. Was the deafness the problem? Is it hard to learn an auditory language when you're deaf. But assuming it can be done, what has been going wrong? Why have the best materials and teachers failed? We think that part of the failure stems from problems connected with cross-cultural communication. We believe that there are misunderstandings between the deaf and hearing cultures that have blocked the kind of attitude and motivation necessary for any learning, especially language learning, to happen between the two cultures. We feel that there is a difference in the *value* that each culture places on English and ASL as communication systems and as survival tools. We feel that deaf peoples' attitudes about themselves, their self-images, are often so poor that these attitudes have contributed to what we see as a "failure syndrome" around the deaf person's learning of English. We feel that language learning is thwarted when a majority culture fails, for whatever reason t,o acknowledge the validity of the minority, when the majority culture is committed to the teaching of its language, while not providing at all for instruction in the minority language. We feel that the problem is related to the interaction between these cultures, not to some innate inability in the deaf person to learn English, not to the deafness *per se*, and not to the failure of materials or teachers.

We believe that cultural difference, when recognized and taken into account in the classroom, can be a very positive force if treated *positively*. We have found that by treating cultural difference as a learning tool in and of itself, we have added greatly to our effectiveness as English teachers. It is difficult to *teach* a language and culture. It is difficult to *learn* a language and culture. What follows is a description of our attempt to reduce that difficulty.

Basic Assumptions and Objectives

Throughout this paper it may come as a surprise to the reader to find English teachers speaking of feelings, attitudes, interests as the basis for learning the English language. But we are three who feel strongly that the affect is a strong and important influence on language learning. It seems to us that English teaching (and education in general) has always implied that to be successful deaf people must in cultural terms become hearing. That is, they must learn the hearing language, must live the hearing lifestyle. And they must do this by denying the validity of any other culture, language, or value system. It is not stated explicitly, but this has always been the message our systems have given to deaf people.

It is the premise of this paper that this "either-or" cultural attitude is dysfunctional for any kind of educational system, and nowhere has it been more detrimental than in the teaching of English to deaf students. That is why we began the approach to teaching English that we used in our classroom in recent years. As our program evolved from a fairly traditional English class, some assumptions we were making became clear:

1. Our students have a language which functions for them—be it ASL or some variation of English.
2. ASL and English are two separate, complete, and valuable languages.
3. English is not a prerequisite to education, intelligence, success, or value as a person.
4. English does not necessarily equal happiness.
5. When two cultures meet, learning happens best in a co-learning, sharing environment.

With these assumptions we were forced to re-think many of our old ideas and reject much of our training as English teachers. We had to develop an entirely new set of affective enabling objectives for our English class, where, of course, the major objective was to help students acquire as much English as possible. In no particular order we wanted to:

1. Establish the fact of two separate and equal languages (ASL and English), two separate cultures (deaf-hearing), and the complete acceptance of both as valid to have or to be.
2. Break down the student's view of themselves as "poor language learners" when, in fact, they already have at least one language, and/or a varia-

tion of a second, and are studying another (standard English).

3. Break down the students' view of themselves as helpless by pointing out the value of what they already have.

4. Overcome the "English equals intelligence" syndrome.

5. Let the students know that it is okay to ask for help—to be wrong.

6. Make it clear that there are options in language learning which the student chooses, including the option not to learn at all.

7. Help students recognize that teachers and students are co-learners—teachers and students are both learning about language and culture.

8. Identify individual learning styles—i.e., which students learn best with a deaf teacher, or a hearing teacher, or from a peer, or alone, or through ASL, or through written exercises.

9. Involve students in planning their learning.

10. Let the students know that we trust their instincts and judgment.

11. Help students develop the skills and attitudes they need to continue the language learning process when they leave our class.

Accomplishing these objectives required changing many attitudes and addressing some common misconceptions about ASL and the deaf culture, about English and the hearing culture, and about language learning. To attain any of them we had to resolve the conflicts that arose between the deaf and hearing cultures by removing ourselves as threats to either one. The strength of our approach has been in our abilities to *function across cultures* easily.

The Approach

Individualizing. Our whole class was based on an individualized approach to learning. This meant that we tried to allocate time and materials according to the needs of our students. We tried to account for different learning styles and paces. Students could even choose the teacher they wanted to work with. To do this, we spent a lot of time at the beginning of each semester diagnosing and planning each individual's program and making adjustments in it throughout the semester. For group work, we also grouped according to need.

Team Teaching. In the Spring of 1976 team teaching began in the English Language Program (ELP) at Gallaudet College almost by accident. Some of us thought it would be a good idea for a new teacher to work closely at first with a more experienced one and Bette, who had been around for awhile, was asked to team with Terry, who had assisted in the program before but was new on the faculty. In the ELP we were all accustomed to assorted students and teachers wandering in and out of our classroom area, so the thought of being under more constant observation by our peers was not too frightening. However, neither of us had ever worked that closely in a class with anyone else, and we were worried about a number of issues. How would we work out our differences in approach and methodology? What would happen if we didn't agree on grading procedures or whether "cuts" counted or on any of the numerous small decisions that are made around any course?

The first time we sat down to talk, it was obvious we would work well together and be able to deal honestly with our disagreements and discomforts. Later, when Tom joined us, the three of us were able to talk to each other with the same openness. We can contribute nothing, therefore, about team teaching where teachers could not harmonize, though we have heard that in schools where teachers are assigned to work together that can become a major problem. What we will describe here was made possible by our smooth working relationship.

When Terry and Bette began that first semester, the benefits of team teaching in an English language class immediately became apparent. What we first noticed is not different from team teaching in any situation. When more than one teacher is working with an individualized course, logistics become infinitely easier. It is possible to schedule students into special groups, to divide and re-divide the class according to individual needs. Each teacher can concentrate on working with one or two specific areas of skill but can also do some joint planning. Since the creativity of two or three persons seems to be more than triple that of one person, more new ideas and materials find their way into the class. Additionally, feedback and reinforcement for the teacher is built into the system, and the team interaction fosters professional development. The three of us have seen each other in every capacity—as lesson planner, materials developer, language resource person, and in every kind of situation—working with large and small groups, and with individuals. As we watched and commented on each other's work, as we planned our class together, we learned a great deal.

Even with two hearing teachers, students seemed to benefit from the team situation in other ways than merely having more materials and more opportunity for group work. Terry and Bette modeled behavior that became the norm in the class. We often asked each other questions, teased each other about not knowing everything. If it was all right for teachers to admit weaknesses and gaps in their knowledge, it became all right for students to do the same. They soon began to ask more questions, to admit freely that they did not know something, and then to ask about it. Terry and Bette dealt with each other as people, not as teachers. We joked, we teased, we had fun. We seriously considered problems together. We shared concerns and successes. We gave each other both positive and negative feedback. We talked about what was happening in our world. Students watched, and then joined the conversations. Soon everyone was joking and teasing and working together. The communication in the classroom felt good.

Sign Behavior. Of course, Terry and Bette signed all the time. We signed when we talked to students and when we talked to each other. When someone else appeared in our class, we signed to the visitor, hearing or deaf, and because it seemed expected, the visitor signed back. We never discussed it. We never pointed it out. But we made clear that communication was a joint responsibility. Our behavior both acknowledged, and ignored, all the cultural differences in the classroom—

deaf/hearing, ASL/English, oral/manual, teacher/student, male/female.

A side benefit of all this was the English language model Terry and Bette were providing. Since we were using Pidgin Sign English when we talked and signed to each other, students had frequent opportunity to "listen in" (eaveslook is the word we like), and they did. Who would miss the chance to find out what the teachers were talking about! Students inevitably picked up some knowledge of conversational English when they were constantly exposed to discussions about familiar and relevant topics. When Terry and Bette worked with a student, we both tried to respond in a language the student understood, whether we were explaining an English grammar structure or talking about the weather. As we switched codes and accommodated ourselves to each language situation, students quickly realized that we valued standard English, and that we accepted a student's language—whatever it was—as a viable communicative tool.

Language and Culture Variation. When Tom joined the team and we became a deaf-hearing team, the impact on students and the benefits of teaming grew immensely. Our teaching team consisted then of three very different people from three very different backgrounds: one comes from a middle-class Presbyterian family in a small northeastern town, one is from a poor Pentecostal family in the back country of South Carolina, and the third grew up in an upper middle-class Jewish home in Brooklyn. As a result, our use of the English language varied widely. Rather than a problem, however, we viewed these differences to be good and healthy, offering a different perspective on life and communication.

This attitude was basic in our classroom. We respected differences of any sort, but especially the language variation that students exhibited. We presumed that whatever language a student was most comfortable using, be it ASL, English, Spanish, or any variation thereof, was good and useful for that person, and was worthy of respect.

We avoided criticizing a student's language. If students felt that theirs was an acceptable language through which they could communicate effectively with those most important to them, then they could begin to see English learning as an opportunity not to begin, but to expand their powers of communication. We did not see ourselves as missionaries bringing light to dark places, communication where there was none before, but as people helping other people understand the vast array of communication skills they already possessed. Having deaf and hearing teachers in the classroom facilitated this process. The first obvious change when Tom joined the team was in the way students related to the teachers. In many instances the more culturally "hearing" students gravitated towards Terry and Bette and the more "deaf" towards Tom. But this was not always true. Some deaf students couldn't accept the expertise and skill of someone deaf (Tom) as an English teacher and initially chose to work with Terry or Bette. Later, we began to watch these barriers crumble.

Modeling. The modeling of behavior in the classroom then gained an added dimension. Terry and Bette had originally been able to model English conversation, openness, how to fill gaps in one's knowledge, and how to handle mistakes. But with Tom on the team, we began to model cross-cultural interaction. It went far beyond simply always signing to each other. What we were able to model is how deaf and hearing people can accept and respond to differences.

Terry and Bette can hear, Tom can't. Tom can use ASL fluently, Bette and Terry can't. So when Terry or Bette needed to know how to say something in ASL, or needed to know a good English translation for a sign, they asked Tom. When we turned on the TV in class to see an important news story, Terry or Bette interpreted. We freely talked about our differences— often. But when one of us needed to know the name of the governor of Connecticut, or how to spell a word, or just what semantic rule could be causing a knotty language problem, we asked either of the others, whoever was nearest or had a moment free. Our actions showed that we considered people around us to be a resources available simply by asking. Our actions also showed our students that we at least recognized our differences—in culture, language skills, and knowledge.

Perhaps as importantly they showed our students that we also recognized and accepted our similarities—in culture, language skills, and knowledge. For students who had constantly been labeled in one way or another as different, handicapped, or deficient, and who had been expected to conform to norms of hearing behavior only, this recognition and acceptance was often startling.

What we were modeling, in one word, was comfort—comfort with difference, comfort with similarity. We joked about these differences and similarities, played with them. We discussed the advantage that goes with being bilingual and when it's a drag to be hearing or deaf. We shared our experiences and frustrations. We were different but we were also the same, and it was clear to our students that our mutual respect and affection and delight in working together had nothing to do with who could hear and who couldn't, who used ASL and who didn't. We were professionals who respected each other's skills and knowledge, friends who enjoyed being with each other, people who liked working in a classroom and learning from each other and our students. We were as alike and different as any three people, and in that context, to hear or not became just one more part of who we were, important because it was, unimportant because it wasn't.

Informal Conversations. Such modeling of behavior can only happen in an accepting, supportive, low-key atmosphere where informal conversations become an important forum for learning. Although it is possible to accomplish this with only one teacher in the classroom, with two or three the task is easier, since the interaction between the teachers themselves sets the tone, provides the model. Conversations in our classroom started in a variety of ways, and we learned to take advantage of them.

Often students asked us the meaning of an English word or sentence, and we explained using as much ASL as we could use effectively. Conversations developed around different ways of expressing a given concept, and how both English and ASL have expressions that are hard to translate. Very often students took the opportunity to teach some ASL to Bette and Terry, who were eager to learn. When we became co-learners, when we learned slowly or forgot easily, our behavior showed students it was okay to be learning a language and okay not to already know it. We found that our interest in ASL alone was enough to initiate many conversations.

It was in informal conversations also that we were best able to counter the "English equals intelligence" syndrome. Many students displayed obvious discomfort, even anger, when we corrected their written English. In response to discovering a common error that the students felt they should have found without the teacher, they often would grimace and call themselves stupid, as evidenced by limited English skills. Students were surprised to realize that we did not consider skill in English as always an appropriate measure of intelligence. Very informally, but very effectively, we used conversations to point out how a person can be brilliant and have poor English, and that calling oneself stupid was not acceptable to us.

How exciting to watch students react to and interact with our team. They quietly picked up our behavior, so that soon many of us together were able to accept and ignore differences and concentrate on other matters. Gradually (in a semester, the modeling seemed to take between six and eight weeks to evoke noticeable impact) we all became individuals, whether hearing or deaf, teacher or student, and different groupings occurred. Students worked with teacher(s) they found compatible, and that was not always based on a deaf/hearing distinction.

As the semester progressed, as the comfort level grew and students began to truly believe that they and their language(s) were accepted, many began almost visibly to relax and ask serious questions about their English language problems, their potential for improving. More students began to share their dismay and frustration with the English language, some to rail at the system which insists they have good English but does not know how to help them get it. Students began to talk about English as a skill they need, not an imposition they must resist. ASL signers began to use it more freely in the classroom; beginning signers worked at communicating. As all this occurred, students who had militantly refused to talk began to use their voices when it erased a communication problem. Students who had always talked, stopped when it was not necessary. Many students settled down to work on English with an absorption they had never felt before.

Using ASL to Teach English—Comparative Analysis. We had noticed that teachers who are fluent users of ASL often use ASL to explain unfamiliar English structures to their students. Carrying this technique a step farther, we began to experiment with comparing and contrasting ASL and English language items. We hoped that this would not only serve to provide a point of reference, a hook for the student to hang a new English structure on, but also to demonstrate graphically that the student is learning *a*—as opposed to *the*—language which, like his/her own, utilizes interesting and even unique structures to express thoughts and feelings.

We found it helpful, for example, to describe the differences in the ways that English and ASL expressed time contexts. We drew comparisons between written English sentences and English glosses of ASL sentences as follows:

ASL	English
YESTERDAY C-E-D-R-I-C DRIVE WASHINGTON	Yesterday Cedric drove to Washington
TOMORROW C-E-D-R-I-C DRIVE WASHINGTON	Tomorrow Cedric will drive to Washington.
C-E-D-R-I-C LIVE WASHINGTON THREE YEARS	Cedric has lived for three years.

We knew that ASL seems to use a time indicator like TODAY, TOMORROW, SINCE, etc., which serves to place the sentence in a particular time frame. There need not be any other marker of time in the sentences until a change in time frame takes place. English uses time words almost optionally, however, and all English verbs must be inflected or marked for tense. Drawing a comparison between the two languages helped the students who knew ASL realize that they already understood and used a temporal concept but that English and ASL employed different language structures to express time.

Recently, while one of us was trying to explain the importance of verb inflection in English, a student asked why in English all verbs had to be marked for tense. After all, she argued, it would be a lot easier for us to use a time word once, like in ASL, and then let that stand until the time frame changed. Although we were unable to answer why English is structured in this way, it was apparent that part of the question was concerned with language redundancy. It was a good opportunity to point out that ASL has its own flukes which are perhaps as inexplicable as those in English, redundancy in reference, for example. We pointed out that the English sentence "He wants a car" is often translated into ASL as HE WANT CAR HE WANT HE, the sentence ending with a copy of the subject of the sentence. ASL has redundancy as does English, but in different ways.

Later on while discussing that many sentences with clauses (The man <u>who I met</u> was blind) can be reduced (The man <u>I met</u> was blind), it became clear that this concept of reduction was also foreign to our students. It was helpful to refer back to our previous discussion, pointing out that the sentence HE WANT CAR HE WANT HE, can be reduced to HE WANT CAR HE or even WANT CAR HE without losing meaning.

Although our experience with this technique is as yet too limited to report on its success, we fell it is a promising vehicle for clarifying the distinctions between ASL and English and for facilitating deaf students' quest for a deeper understanding of the nature of their bilingualism. The findings recently made and yet to be made by linguists studying ASL also promise to make this method of English instruction increasingly more attractive.

Using ASL to Teach English—ASL Videotapes. In 1975–1977, Astrid Goodstein and Barbara Kannapell, both native users of ASL, developed two sets of videotape lessons that use

ASL to teach English vocabulary and "idioms." Each lesson consists of a pre-test, practice exercises, and a post-test. Both the pre- and post-tests contain approximately seven ASL sentences, each of which has translations into English. For the pre-test, the ASL sentences are presented on the videotape and students respond with a written English translation of the ASL sentence. Based on their performance on the pre-test, students elect to proceed through the lesson.

For the exercises in each lesson the ASL sign or signs are given English translations, then three or four example sentences are given for both the ASL vocabulary item and the English translation. Students are able to watch the ASL, which they understand, translated into English in several example sentences.

Students' responses to the ASL videotapes were strongly favorable, especially during the first few showings. The first reaction of many students was outright laughter, presumably from the strangeness and surprise of seeing ASL in as formal a place as an English vocabulary lesson. For some students the ASL videotape lessons became the only friendly and comfortable materials in our entire program.

The ASL tapes had the direct impact of presenting ASL and English as different but equal languages. The tone is one of respect and dignity for both languages. By paralleling written English and signed ASL, the value and function of each is made clear. Students feel that they are owners of one and part-owners of the other. Suddenly the task of acquiring English is seen as a process of expressing oneself in a different way, not just expressing oneself.

Some persons have remarked that deaf teachers seem to have more success with the tapes, perhaps because of greater facility in ASL. It may also be that students are more comfortable with deaf teachers in the presence of ASL, at least until a greater trust level has been built between teachers and students. We found the comfort level of students to be of great importance in the use of these materials, since the informal discussions that occur as a result are probably of greater value than the English vocabulary learned. Inevitably students get into discussions of language differences and variations, arguing about various translations and meanings.

Language Consultation.

A. Teacher/Student

When students feel good about themselves as learners and decide that they wish to improve their English skills, the basic nature of the teacher/student relationship changes dramatically. The teacher ceases to be an omnipotent being with all the answers, and becomes instead a resource for a student bent on getting the skills he/she wants. Responsibility for learning is placed squarely where it should be: in the hands of the student. Students cease to be passive reproducers of pattern drills, and become active, discerning educational consumers.

This becomes especially important if second language learning is seen as a life-long process. What good does it do if students need to be "taught" when they are to continue to acquire English? Not many of us have seen students leave our classes with all the English they will need to communicate effectively in that language. Why then do we insist that they do only what we tell them to do? It would seem even more important to help students develop the attitude and learn the processes necessary for them to seek out and acquire English without us—than to teach the skills themselves.

In our program we attempted to build a teacher/student relationship where students used teachers as language consultants. In consultation with one of us, students created their own English language objectives, selected materials, and determined their own grades. We suggested, encouraged, and reinforced, but all of the important decisions were made by the students themselves.

In a very real way when students are in control of their own language learning, they become the orchestrators of their own education. Since we no longer made basic decisions for students, we were available to be used by students to accomplish their objectives. Though difficult at the beginning for most students, and impossible ever for some, by the middle of the first semester nearly all the students were making daily decisions about which materials to use, whether to use a teacher to answer questions or explain unfamiliar terms, or electing to join teacher-centered activities (such as structure lectures or reading groups).

We found in these consultations that we could reinforce the idea of language variation. It was productive for us to avoid using words like "wrong" or drawing large red "x's" through non-English items in a writing sample, explaining to the student instead that what he/she was trying to say is not generally said that way in English. Where possible, we tried to point out when he/she had written ASL in English gloss. For example, if a student wrote "Yesterday Cedric finish Botany paper," we would mention that this is perfectly acceptable when signed but that in English, it is necessary to show the past in the verb.

B. Student/Student

It is ridiculous, of course, to suggest that students at Gallaudet came to us with no language consultation skills. In the dorm they very quickly found out who could read well when they couldn't read the directions on a take-home exam or a form for financial aid. And even before asking help from one of the Resident Assistants in the dorm or a teacher, they often would ask a roommate or classmate. Peers are excellent language consultants, not only because they are convenient, but quite probably because they use the same language.

In our English class, students would usually only ask questions or help of the teacher at the beginning of the year. As time went on, however, students often tired of waiting for teachers who were working with other students, and would ask peers for assistance. It took no time at all for students to identify other students with better English skills in their class who would help when asked. In some cases students so much preferred peer consultation that they approached a teacher only when there was no one else to get the information from, or if no one else knew. We worried a bit at first that peer consultation might lead to erroneous ideas or misconceptions; people enter our program, after all, by virtue of their apparent weakness in English. We were right. Often they *were* given incorrect information. Learning who, and when to trust in a consulting relationship, however, is a valuable skill to learn. We encouraged student/student language consultation as much as possible.

C. *Teacher/Teacher*

Perhaps one of the reasons why we feel language consultation is so beneficial, is that we found it to be immensely helpful for ourselves. Having another teacher or two in an informal classroom atmosphere made it possible for us to ask each other for help when we encountered something we were unsure of or uncomfortable with. We were able to draw on each other's strengths, and thereby provide a model for language consultation to our students. The dynamics of this consultative relationship was explained in the earlier discussion of our team teaching.

Reaction of Students to Seeing ASL in an Academic Setting

One of the most compelling reasons for including ASL in the English classroom is the reaction of the ASL-using students when it is introduced. At first there is the cynicism of disbelief. No one believes that ASL is an academic language. No one believes that an English teacher would actually defend ASL as a language. Everyone believes to some degree that ASL is the culprit responsible for the English problems of deaf people. The *reason* deaf people have bad English is *because* they learn ASL and *therefore* ignore English.

But at the same time, in the love-hate relationship with ASL, everyone who uses it believes that ASL is the easiest, most comfortable means of communication. They believe that most of the everyday needs of deaf people are met through ASL. None of them is willing for a minute to give up ASL if that were possible. They are fiercely possessive of this language that is so important in their lives.

So when ASL was discussed openly and seriously in our discussions about languages and language attitudes, when myths about ASL were forcefully dispelled, when ASL was used comparatively and on par with English, when one of the teachers preferred ASL in his English classroom, and when the other two teachers were not threatened by ASL in their English classroom, the student hardly knew what to think. But this confusion was short-lived. After the initial shock our students quickly learned that anything having to do with ASL and other language variations was appropriate for our classroom. When they saw ASL on the videotapes, for example, they were initially confused, then fascinated, finally able to take an active part in critiquing the tapes and the translations.

Students were slightly disbelieving of a *deaf* English teacher. They were even more disbelieving of a deaf English teacher *using ASL*. What kind of trickery was this? It took some students an entire semester to discover that Terry was hearing and that Tom was deaf—why? Because Terry often used ASL and because Tom behaved very much like a hearing person at times. Watching this functioning across cultures was the most effective stereotype-buster of all. The look of realization on the faces of students who discovered that the ASL they were using has pronouns, tense markers, and word order had to rate as proof of one of the all-time greatest learning experiences. The concept of self as an effective language user and learner was harder to swallow for most of the students and many resisted this idea until some time after leaving our class. It was hard for many to accept that after all these years they are suddenly not "language deficient" and more so simply because three English teachers said so. And rightly so. But most, if not all, began to think and to question old knowledge and attitudes and wonder if perhaps we were right. It was this opening up, this searching for new answers to questions about the deaf culture and ASL, about English and language learning, that we witnessed in our classroom, that made it all a success in our eyes.

Success on an Individual Level—Some Case Studies

The few examples we have space to describe we hope can convey some of the excitement we felt about so many of our students (we have, of course, changed their names).

Joe arrived bitter and disgusted. Top of his class in his state school, he was appalled to discover how weak his English skill really was. He came to us during our first semester together, before we had developed many of our more formal materials and methods. But we knew immediately we would not push him into any work he did not want to do. We were all aware of and sensitive to his feeling of helplessness, even despair, at ever improving. We tried. We talked about the difficult nature of language acquisition, especially for adults. We talked about how not knowing English did not mean he was dumb. We talked to him personally about any number of issues—sports, politics, etc.—as an equal. Still, we never felt as if we had succeeded. When he left our class, his English was not appreciably better, and we had no indication that his attitude had changed much either, although he had stopped griping as much.

Eighteen months later, the English Department offered an English skills course for credit for the first time, and Joe was one of the first to enroll. His teacher commented repeatedly about the enthusiasm and determination that he displayed, as well as his improved self-esteem.

We have no proof, but we would like to think that the changes Joe exhibited began in our classroom. We would like to think that the atmosphere of acceptance allowed him to begin to separate his English skill from his concept of self-worth, and to begin to see himself as a skilled person who could take control of his own education.

Then there was Sally—militantly deaf, militantly ASL, who never used her voice, and who would only work with Tom. When she needed assistance, she would always wait until he was free, even if that meant waiting until the next class. The only group she responded positively to was Tom's ASL videotape group, where discussion revolved around the different ways English and ASL expressed similar concepts. We never pushed, we never insisted, and gradually she began, cautiously, to join in informal conversations with Terry and Bette. We often had trouble understanding her, which at the beginning thoroughly disgusted her. As time went on, her disgust eased to mere impatience, and eventually turned to acceptance. Finally one day when Bette's back was turned, she heard her name called in an unknown voice. It was Sally, who from then on worked hard at communicating, and worked well with all of us.

We suspect that Sally's turnabout was due to a build-up of trust—trust that we valued her as a person, that we did not judge her on the basis of her English skill, and that we were honestly willing to let her be in control of her own language learning.

Not all students came to us turned off. Ed, who was older and had a family, had given up his job to come to Gallaudet. He was ready to learn English, impatient with himself for not knowing enough, ready to do what we told him. We didn't tell him. We used our best consulting skills; we gave him as many options as we could; we helped him identify his strengths and weaknesses. We worked on building his confidence in his ability to learn. When he left us, he continued working on his English, both voluntarily and in the credit class. Our trust, respect, and willingness to help him get what he wanted all contributed to what we thought was a reasonable objective: We didn't turn him off to learning English; we reinforced his own determination to get it.

Finally, there was Susan, representative of many students. She came to us late in the semester, a transfer from another class. She worked almost completely independently, which gave her less personal contact with us as others had. Still, she had been with us for nearly two months when she called Tom, who did not respond since his back was turned. She tried calling him again, ignoring a classmate who told her Tom was deaf. When Bette concurred that Tom was indeed deaf, she was met by a stare of frank disbelief. Susan was at last able to get Tom's attention and asked him if he were deaf. His affirmative response was still unacceptable, so she stated that surely he was hard of hearing. Words cannot describe the shock it was for Susan to hear that no, he was not hard of hearing; he was deaf. Susan's assumptions about cultural boundaries and the world of language learning could not include deaf English teachers (any more, presumably than it could have included hearing ASL users). One was either deaf or English speaking, and her experience with Tom brought home a whole new concept: that bilingualism/biculturalism is a reality. We hope she left us at the end of the semester feeling that it may be a real possibility for *her* as well.

Our Own Feelings About The Approach

We each, of course, feel quite differently about what we did. Our own differences, cultural and other, led us to different experiences and learnings. But we do share some basic perceptions.

We were all aware as we went along of the risks involved. We were apprehensive about working together, about allowing feelings and attitudes into the classroom, about trying our new materials and methods. We were anxious about losing traditional teacher control, about actually giving students responsibility for their own learning instead of just talking about the theory. However, as each step in the process led to the next, as we took greater risks, we began to feel the benefits.

We all feel more successful as teachers. Because we defined success as beginning a process as well as ending it, we felt good when we saw a student take the first step towards learning English—a step which simply might have been realizing that he/she was a good person—even without the English he/she was seeking. We are all convinced that team teaching is not only effective, but lots of fun as well.

We are convinced that much of the success we have felt in the classroom has grown out of the nature of the team itself. We were different, so we sought out our differences and as we held them up to be admired and respected, we learned from them. It didn't matter that Terry couldn't lead a good discussion group, or Bette couldn't reach the TV.monitor on the wall, or Tom couldn't use a voice phone. We learned that we were all complete, though in different ways. We not only expected our *students* to become more bilingual and more bicultural and to increase their cross-cultural skills; we expected these things from *ourselves* as well. We modeled self-confident co-learning behaviors and felt rewarded when we saw those behaviors grow in our students.

We realize, of course, that we were luckier than most English language teachers in that we were located in a center where deaf/hearing issues were discussed intensively, where we had easy contact with linguists working on the analysis of ASL, and where, most importantly, there were some deaf teachers. We cannot stress too greatly the significance of having deaf teachers in the English classroom. Tom's presence alone, in an environment that students seemed to feel belonged only to others not of their own culture, was a learning experience, as it pointed out boldly that deaf people and English are not irreconcilably alien. When there is a deaf teacher who is skilled in and respectful of ASL, English, and all variations, then there is greater learning. When there is a classroom that has both deaf and hearing teachers with skills in and respect for ASL, English, and all variations, a profound interest in working across cultures and obvious respect for each other, then there is an opportunity for new understandings. Such an environment provides fertile ground for beginning a process which seems to result not only in students learning more language but in students who feel good about doing it.

There are, of course, far too few bilingual deaf or hearing teachers in English classrooms to staff all the English language programs for deaf students in this country. Finding, hiring, and training deaf and hearing people to provide positive linguistic, cross-cultural models in English language programs is perhaps the greatest challenge we face.

15

STUCK in School: Meaning and Culture in a Deaf Education Classroom

Sherman Wilcox

> The subject may appear an insignificant one, but we shall see that it possesses some interest; and the maxim "de minimis lex non curat" [the law is not concerned with trifles] does not apply to science.
>
> Charles Darwin, *"The Formation of Vegetable Mould, Through the Action of Worms, With Observations on Their Habits."*

A Sign and Its Uses.

IN DISCUSSING Darwin's last treatise, Stephen Jay Gould notes that it was frequently through the study of apparently insignificant details that the great natural historian was able to formulate a general scientific theory. Darwin's theory of natural selection, though a description of the evolution of life, was based on local adaptation. As Gould notes, one of the most productive theories of life in general originated from the notion that "order in nature arises as a coincidental by-product of struggle among individuals" (Gould 1982).

I believe that a close examination of behavioral and linguistic data in deaf education, seeming trifles in the overall scheme of American deaf education, can likewise provide interesting insights. I will argue that a detailed and cognitively motivated analysis of one such "trifle" can add to our knowledge about the ways in which students make sense of what's happening in the classroom. I will also suggest that this accomplishment, the sense made, is very much a product of the culture of American Deaf education.

The trifle I will describe and analyze here began during the 1981-82 school year at Northfield High School[1]; it consisted of the greatly increased use of the American Sign Language (ASL) lexical item generally glossed STUCK. The use of this sign reached its peak during the 1982-83 school year. At the time of writing (fall of 1983-84 school year) the use of STUCK was rapidly declining and only rarely observed.

In most ASL dictionaries and student texts the sign glossed STUCK usually is taken to refer to a situation in which some person or thing is caught in a problem and has no way out (i.e. the meaning is derived):

> Stuck: having a problem and not being sure how to solve it. (Madsen 1982).

> STUCK: CAUGHT-IN-THE-ACT, v. phrase
> CHOKE, v.n.
> STRANDED, adj.
> TRAP, n.v.   (Sternberg 1981)

> 1. (A deaf club will have a meeting to elect new officers. The former president served for four years, but recently died. Now the deaf are stuck): NOW DEAF STUCK. (Madsen 1982).

---

[1] All names are fictitious; quotations from students are given in free translation.

2. (Pat asks Lee if he went to a meeting. She says it was terrific and if he missed it there is no one to blame but himself. Lee replies that he knows that but says that he was stuck because of his job): KNOW-THAT, ME, STUCK J-O-B. (Baker & Cokely 1980).

All these are examples of the traditional use of STUCK. The students at Northfield give similar examples of this usage:

3. YOUR TRUCK STUCK IN M-U-D.
4. YOU FORGOT BOOK, STUCK.
5. ME STUCK, ME CAN'T GO ASSEMBLY.
6. I AM STUCK BECAUSE NOT ENOUGH CHAIRS.
7. I AM STUCK IN ELEVATOR.
8. B-U-L-L-D-O-Z-E-R STUCK B-Y SNOW.

However, it is not in any of these senses that the sign STUCK was being used in the phenomenon described here. The deaf students, modifying the semantics of STUCK, used it in the following way:

9. (Discussing the deaf students in the program, whom the student knows much better than the teacher) Student: I know all, STUCK.

10. TEACHER: That problem is wrong. The answer is '14'.
STUDENT: No. That's right, '12'!
TEACHER: No; I think you got it wrong. You see, you did it wrong right here, where you ... oh ... oh, yeah; that's right, '12' is the right answer.
STUDENT: STUCK!

Freely translated, this version of the sign STUCK means 'I got you.' Roughly comparable hearing expressions would be "chop, shafted, burn," or more recently, "face." The problem is to describe the details of this semantic extension of STUCK.

The study of the relation between semantics and culture has traditionally been a task in the ethnography of cognitive systems. It is an attempt to "discern how people construe their world of experience from the way they talk about it" (Frake

1980a). Given the traditional models of language available, this task has not been an easy one. Basso (1976) has noted the inadequacies of traditional grammar. Langacker (1983) has proposed a cognitive grammar as better able to meet these demands.

In the traditional use of STUCK (the dictionary, text, and student usage examples 3-8), something or someone is literally caught in something (like mud) or figuratively caught in a problem or situation. Also the user of the sign may be the "stickee" or may report that someone else or something is stuck.

The non-traditional use of STUCK at Northfield introduces another element into the relationship and the underlying syntax. The student in example 10 above signs only "STUCK," but the meaning is, 'I defeated you.' In terms of semantic-based grammar, STUCK is no longer process only with what is stuck as patient; it is action-process and has an agent as well. In terms of Langacker's cognitive grammar, the focus in the traditional usage is on what is stuck, the person with the job or the truck in the mud. But in the Northfield usage, the focus is on the agent, the person doing the sticking. Prototypically this is a student. Any other person can be "stuck," but the students agree that if the stickee is a hearing teacher, STUCK carries more punch.

To summarize the claims made about the semantic extension of STUCK:

> 1. STUCK always focuses attention on the person I have called the stickor; this is the active person in the relational profile of STUCK.

> 2. STUCK symbolizes an active process rather than a stative relation or passive, completed process; it does not describe, it does something. The agent or subject is typically a deaf student; the landmark, patient, object is likewise a hearing teacher.

To support these claims, I will offer evidence in three areas: paralinguistics (i.e. the body posturing and sounds co-occurring with production of the sign STUCK); the morphological processes of ASL; and the folk etymology of STUCK at Northfield.

The production of STUCK is accompanied by a characteristic body posture, facial activity, and sometimes by the noise of the hand striking the chest as STUCK is produced. The body posture, characteristic of aggressive behavior, includes leaning forward, protruding the chest, pulling the shoulders back, raising the head, and jutting out the chin.[2] The facial expression includes squinting the eyes and knitting the brow. The lips are tightly pursed and curved up in an apparent smirk. The body language thus seems to be saying, 'Watch out for me; I'm powerful and won't hesitate to use it against you.' (STUCK of course is the metaphorical use of this power.) The noise from the blow on the signer's chest emphasized the aggressive nature of this sign, and all these cues parallel nicely the changes in the semantic structure of STUCK. Semantically, the power of STUCK resides in the trajector, which is the speaker, In production, STUCK is accompanied by behaviors that emphasize the aggressive power of that speaker.[3]

The traditional signing of STUCK uses a short, sharp, tense, or checked movement (Stokoe et al. 1976). At Northfield, this is the movement of STUCK signed in traditional use. The extended sense, however, is signed with a long unrestrained movement, generally starting with the arm fully outstretched in front of the signer (and so well into the addressee's personal space). This of course accords with what Klima and Bellugi

---

[2] Wescott (1971) claims that aggressive behavior is more iconic than most animal behaviors, and for this reason may be understood by other species.

[3] Osgood (1971) found that power plays an important role in the semantic structure of over 30 languages from various cultures. To compare the semantic structures of STUCK on three dimensions of meaning identified by Osgood:

	trad. STUCK	extend. STUCK
evaluation	bad/unfavorable	good/favorable
activity	inactive	active
potency	weak	strong

(1979) have found, that changes in the "movement parameter" signal semantic changes.

Finally, the folk etymology of STUCK provides more support for the claim I am making. The deaf students have a story about when and where STUCK in this sense was created and who created it. According to this folk story, STUCK was invented in 1981 in the classroom of one of the hearing-impaired teachers.[4] Significantly, this teacher was the least skilled in signing of all the teachers in the deaf education program. (She had been a teacher in an oral program for many years but was making an effort to accept and learn Signed English.) The students even tell stories about the originator of this use of STUCK. When I asked the one they identified who invented this sign, he replied: "You're looking at him. I did it in Miss Smith's class."

The deaf students have strong intuitions about when, where, and how to use STUCK. They recognize that this sign is distinct from the sign in its traditional meanings or even such derived meanings as 'pregnant out of wedlock'. They are also aware that until recently the staff did not fully understand the meaning of this use of STUCK. During the period in which the sign was used most rampantly at Northfield, staff members assumed that it meant something similar to 'pregnant,' although they report being puzzled about how this meaning made sense in the context of the actual use. One teacher recalled thinking at the time, "Why are they saying pregnant? I'm not pregnant!" When it became obvious that 'pregnant' did not quite capture the meaning of STUCK, the staff members concluded that

---

[4] Whether this use of STUCK was truly "created" at Northfield (i.e. never used before in this sense), is not a question here. The point is that the deaf students at Northfield report that they definitely recognized the difference between traditional STUCK and extended STUCK and had never seen the latter before. This claim is substantiated by the experience of one student. He had spent his elementary and mid-school years at the state school for the deaf with many of the students now at Northfield, but he had lived in California in 1980-81. When he returned and entered Northfield, he remembers seeing stuck used in its extended sense and being puzzled about what it meant. He said he "watched people use it, analyzed it, and talked to people about it. Then I understood."

whatever it meant it was not nice. Consequently, many out-lawed STUCK in their classrooms, and some even went so far as to forbid STUCK In their presence anywhere. STUCK eventually spread to the mid-school deaf education program, where it was determined by the teachers to be a "dirty sign" and forbidden.

The students agree that although STUCK was used on peers (this was probably the most frequent use), it was much more satisfying to use it on a teacher. One student explained later: "It's like the teacher, counselors, principals—whoever—are higher than me. But I can make them wrong, those high up people. STUCK!"

Not all the students were willing to be caught doing this, of course. Those who did were labeled trouble makers. Informal statistics gathered from discussions with the students reveal that of those students rated highest as trouble makers by their peers, the majority were boys who also rated high as users of STUCK. In the students' judgments STUCK may not be a "dirty word," but it certainly marks one socially. STUCK is a demonstration of a lack of respect for authority.

The claim here is that the deaf students at Northfield exhibited linguistic creativity in modifying the semantics of the common lexical item STUCK. This derived form of STUCK emphasizes action and focuses attention on the aggressive power of the student. It is now necessary to study the contextual factors surrounding this change of meaning. Change does not occur in a vacuum; meaning is not unrelated to the real world. As Langacker notes:

> Every experience (linguistic or otherwise) that some-how involves a notion has an impact on our understanding of this notion and consequently on the meaning of an expression designating it... [these impacts] are the determinants of semantic structure. (1983: 167)

In the next section I will examine the possible connections between the changes in the semantic structure of STUCK and the real world situation that undoubtedly sanctioned them.

The Sign's Cultural Context.

Northfield is a large high school (enrollment 2500) within the Northfield Public School system. It was chosen as the primary site for the high school mainstream program for hearing-impaired students in the system. With a few exceptions, every high-school age hearing-impaired student in the area attends Northfield. The staff of the program currently consists of four teachers (three of whom are certified in deaf education), three full-time certified interpreters, four educational aides, and one speech and language therapist who is assigned full time to the program. Although skills vary widely, all the staff in the program can sign.

At the time that STUCK began to appear at Northfield, the staff situation was much the same. Indeed the staff at Northfield throughout this time was not unlike the staff in most deaf education, mainstream programs across the country. The level of education was high. The signing ability ranged from adequate to good proficiency in Signed English. At various times hearing persons of deaf parents were employed as aides; at no time, however, were there any deaf persons on the Northfield staff. Until recently all staff members of the hearing-impaired program were female.

The deaf student body at Northfield consists of some students who have spent their entire educational career in public school programs and also of a substantial number of "transfers" from the state school for the deaf. As a matter of fact, these transfer students led to a substantial increase in enrollment in both the mid-school mainstream program and the Northfield (high school) program during the period covered in this report.

Descriptive statistics concerning the students' signing ability, schooling, and other characteristics were not formally collected, but informal discussions with the students revealed these facts about the hearing-impaired student population:

39 total; 24 male., 15 female.

26 able to "use ASL"[5]
19 attended state school previously at least part of a
    year (many in residential schools only)
10 had other deaf family members
33% could be labeled "trouble makers"

This last item needs further discussion. To state it simply, there was a dramatic rise in behavior problems, drug and sex related problems, and student-teacher tension in the deaf education program during the period from late 1980 to early 1983. Of several factors, three are important here: the physical setting, the transfer situation, and teacher-student interactions.

1. Until recently the entire deaf education program was housed in two mobile barracks outside the main complex at Northfield. With the exception of the mainstream classes, the students had all their classes in these barracks. Students and teachers alike were forced into a cramped physical situation.

2. The transfer of nineteen of these students, who had been most of their time in residential school settings, was the result of student decisions, parental decisions, and suspensions of students from the state school Those who transferred on their own reported that problems in the dormitory had led to this choice, and they claimed that the education at the state school was better, but that the extra-curricular situation was unsatisfactory. Some of the students came to Northfield because their parents wanted them to attend public school and live at home. The improved services (e.g. certified interpreters) in the public school system made this a viable option for parents. Finally, several of the students had been suspended from the state school for behavior problems, in most cases drug abuse. The staff at Northfield was unprepared for these students and their problems. Even in the best of circumstances transferring to a large public school can be a traumatic experience for a deaf students. These were not the best of circumstances.

---

[5]The students who contributed to this discussion had also participated in many discussions about the nature of ASL and the difference between this language and other signing systems. Thus, I regard their intuitions about who signed ASL and who did not to be accurate.

Students in the state school for the deaf lead lives relatively isolated from the modern world of the public school. Their extracurricular life is also much more controlled than is the typical high school student's. They were faced at Northfield with considerably more open sexual and drug-related activities, and many of them wound up in serious drug trouble. These and sex-related problems were often brought into the classroom. Of course the same unfamiliarity with "freedom" leading to problems at school also created problems at home. In summary, the transfer students were unprepared for the life awaiting them outside the school for the deaf. Support services to aid in this transition were not readily available in the public schools. Many parents sought these services elsewhere. Nevertheless, the extent of the culture shock brought on by transfer had considerable effect on the deaf education program at Northfield.

3. Finally, teacher-student interaction had much to do with the situation in which the cultural-semantic phenomenon discussed here arose. Many, perhaps most, interactions between hearing teachers and deaf students proceed smoothly and facilitate the educational process. However, this is not always the case. Two factors seem to cause troubled interactions, linguistic miscommunication and the political and cultural aspects of deaf education.

There is a growing number of studies that support the notion that to understand deaf education we must view it from a bilingual-bicultural perspective (e.g. Caccamise & Hicks 1980, Charrow & Wilbur 1975, Erting 1978, Kannapell 1974, 1980, Woodward 1982). The linguistic and cultural situation in deaf education is exceedingly complex. For many of the deaf students at Northfield, American Sign Language is the vernacular: their world, what is important in their everyday lives both in and out of school, is largely conceived and communicated through this language; however, because of various factors (see Woodward 1982), ASL was virtually unrecognized as having any significant role in education at Northfield.

For these and other reasons, I believe it is accurate to describe what happens in many interactions of deaf with hearing persons as interethnic miscommunication.[6] Interethnic miscommunication has been described by linguists and anthropologists (Erickson & Shultz 1982, Gumperz 1982a & b, Scollon & Scollon 1981), and it is a major factor in a leading theory of multicultural education, the cultural difference model (McDermott 1982).

The students at Northfield corroborate this claim. They report that they frequently have trouble understanding the teachers. Sometimes, they say, teachers will sign in a way that they cannot understand. Sometimes the teachers don't understand, or misunderstand, the students' signing. At least one teacher resorted to writing notes when giving explanations of required class assignments. Sometimes this miscommunication is not so much a matter of understanding what is being said as of understanding why the student is saying it. Surely this struggle to "make sense" is equally difficult for the deaf student. The usual result is that the students become frustrated and give up trying to communicate. Some even become unwilling to communicate.

Given these circumstances, it is easy for teachers to assume that the students are unable to communicate. If the deaf education classroom can be characterized as a bilingual-bicultural setting, then the model of bicultural education that has

---

[6]An article by Robert C. Johnson in the Fall 1983 Gallaudet Research Institute Newsletter summarizes the recently completed study by Carol Erting, with the subtitle "An anthropological analysis of interaction among parents, teachers, and deaf children in a preschool." Erting suggests (1) teachers' implicit attitude that English is superior to ASL, and (2) an apparent inability of hearing people to maintain a visual rather than an auditory orientation to communication when speaking and signing, may lead to linguistic and cultural conflicts similar to those here called (after Scollon) interethnic miscommunication. She notes that this phenomenon may begin as early as preschool and finds a "dynamic tension" resulting from conflicting influences of Deaf and hearing cultures. She describes one hearing teacher thus: "... her interaction resembles a performance more than the finely-tuned communicative interaction so necessary for promoting linguistic and cognitive development." Erting concludes that educators must seek a better balance between English instruction and instruction in Deaf culture and the deaf experience.

been operating in the United States for 150 years and continues as strongly as ever is the cultural deficit model (McDermott 1982).

The deficit model asserts that children not learning in school have been broken by impoverished experiences; they are broken kids. The theory of learning that this model espouses is that knowledge merely enters the kids' heads from without. The best educational strategy for these kids in this view is to intervene, the earlier the better, and to make them whole again.

The results of following this deficit model of bicultural education have been described by the Brazilian educator Paulo Freire (1970). He sees the model in the more general frame of oppression, and I believe that some features of his description are appropriate to the situation at Northfield and to deaf education in general. He sees the teacher-student relationship developed in the deficit model of education as basically a relationship of oppression. He terms the oppressors Subjects, those who know and act. They have a paternalistic attitude toward their students and feel they must make them into images of themselves. They do violence to their students because "violence is initiated by those who oppress, who exploit, who fail to recognize others as persons..." (Freire 1970). The oppressed are Objects in the educational process in Freire's view; they are known by the teachers (who assume they know their "Objects" better than the students know themselves) and are acted on by the teachers. The oppressed are considered in this view the pathology of the healthy society, and because they are things to be turned into images of the oppressors, they "...live in the duality in which to be is to be like, and to be like is to be like the oppressor..." (Freire 1970:33). This verbal image bears a remarkable resemblance to a picture by the deaf artist Betty Miller (Figure 1).

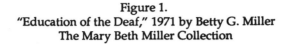

Figure 1.
"Education of the Deaf," 1971 by Betty G. Miller
The Mary Beth Miller Collection

According to this theory of education and of what goes on in students' heads (or what does not), the pedagogy of education is the act of depositing. The students are at best empty containers, at worst broken copies of normal people, and they need to be fixed and filled. Since in this view there is nothing worthwhile in the students' heads, there is no need to consult them. Others have noted the situation Freire describes in deaf education, notably Woodward, who finds the roots of the oppression in "the Hearing ethnocentric view that Deaf adults are isolated pathological individuals instead of culturally different members of a suppressed minority group" (1982: 30).

To begin with, the situation at Northfield is not called "deaf education" by those engaged in it; their term is "hearing-impaired education." The teachers are quick to point this out to anyone who speaks of "the deaf program" (even when the speaker is one of the program staff). The students, of course, call themselves "Deaf," and they make a sharp distinction between those who are Deaf and those who are deaf. This distinction, "Deaf" for a culturally defined group and "deaf" for an audiological defined group, is taken from Padden (this volume). When a newsletter was begun by staff members of several hearing-impaired programs in the school system to which Northfield High belongs, not surprisingly it was called the "Hearing-Impaired Newsletter." In the fall of 1983, when an all-student run newsletter was started by one of the teachers, the students unanimously voted that it should be called the "Northfield Deaf Pride." The teachers, it seems, are categorizing the students in terms of their inability to be hearing people. The deaf students, on the other hand, categorize each other in terms of cultural affiliations. Deaf students are those who use ASL and associate with each other; the others (most often called "hard-of-hearing") typically speak English and associate mostly with hearing people.

In the eyes of staff members at Northfield, language is the area in which their students are most deficient. One frequently hears teachers discussing a student's language in these terms: "Oh, he has very poor language;" or "Yes; James has almost no language." Of course, what is meant here is that students rarely have proficiency in English, either spoken, written, or signed. The ASL skills of the majority of Deaf students at Northfield are a joy to behold, but these skills, while not actively suppressed, are not recognized as valuable in the educational endeavor. ASL skills will not, after all, get deaf students jobs. As one staff member put it, "We have to make these students understand the importance of English."

This emphasis on English is also reflected in the language curriculum developed by the staff for use in all hearing-impaired programs in the Northfield public school system. The 150-page document consistently equates language skills with English skills. ASL is never mentioned.

It would be unfair to place the responsibility for this situation totally on the hearing teachers. These teachers are the products of teacher education programs that typically do not even require proficiency in Signed English, let alone American Sign Language. Also, administrators of deaf education programs, both in state schools for the deaf and in mainstream programs, hold negative attitudes toward bilingualism and bicultural education. For example, in a survey of experts in the field of deaf education, the acceptance of bilingualism ranked 42.5 out of 48, and the importance of hiring more Deaf teachers ranked even lower, 45 out of 48 (Woodward 1982).

Deaf students are sensitive to this ignoring of their linguistic and cultural heritage. The students at Northfield do not frame their thought on this in these cultural terms. They do, however, have thoughts about the place of ASL and Deaf culture in their education. One student, for example, explained that:

> Some people have decided that English has to be used at Northfield. But deaf people when they are out and around, at home, at play, or talking to friends, like to use ASL. I only know ASL. I know I have to use English for things like writing papers, but I hate English signing. I like ASL. ASL is easy to understand.

Another student was adamant about his preference for ASL, yet he was also concerned about his English proficiency, which he knew would be important later when he attended college:

> I feel that ASL is more interesting and expressive. I know that English is very important and it is good to have experience with English. But some teachers don't like ASL; they think it is bad and they love English. When teachers use signed English I don't understand. But some teachers are really skilled in both ASL and English. When a teacher uses

ASL to explain English, it makes it easy for me to want to
learn and write English.

Concerning the place of Deaf culture and Deaf people in
education, this same student said, "I wish a deaf teacher could
be in charge of the hearing-impaired program. A person like
that could be skilled in ASL and English!"

When one staff member started framing these questions
and concerns in terms of culture, the students became quite in-
trigued and were able in a short time to make significant
contributions to this discussion of ASL and Deaf culture. But
like ASL, Deaf culture is not part of the hearing-impaired curriculum. What exposure the students do get to their own
language and culture comes "subversively" in such classes as
World Concepts or Language Arts.

The picture that develops of the situation at Northfield is
that of poor communication between teacher and student, and
of a lack of understanding on the part of the staff, both of the
culture shock faced by deaf students who are suddenly removed from a protective, isolating environment and placed in
the open environment of the modern public school, and of lack
of awareness of and respect for deaf students as linguistically
and culturally different. It was a situation in which the deaf
students were, quite literally, stuck in school. From this
environment STUCK emerged.

The Sign as Event.

> Every situation in life, as it is experienced, can be de-
> fined by reference to one or more events that can be con-
> strued to encompass it and to lend meaning to what occurs
> within it...[C]ulture provides principles for framing experi-
> ence as eventful in particular ways...(Frake 1980b)

STUCK is more than merely a word to describe the state
of being unable to speak or respond. It is an event, a happening.
And it is an event that is very much situated within the overall
environment of the deaf education program just described. The
sign itself offers a window into the deaf students' cognitive or-

ganization of their environment. STUCK, we might say, is a symbolic unit that provides a point of access into a complex cognitive network.

According to Frake, society is organized for the production of social occasions or "scenes." Major social institutions like religion and education can in this view be considered "organizations for the production of scenes of the same type" (Frake 1980b). What is a social occasion? Frake used the example of a "talk"—a talk is a social occasion that occurs in a certain setting and is organized along certain dimensions. It is what we would tell someone if they sat down beside us and asked, "What's happening here?" It is an example of a "conceptual unit whereby we organize our memories of experience in formulating accounts of what is happening, our memories of what has happened, and our predictions and plans for what will happen" (Frake 1980b: 57).

Social occasions are organized along certain dimensions of cultural structure. A talk, for example, is organized along the dimensions of formality (a talk is more formal that a class) and risk (in a talk the speaker faces some risk and the audience can relax, but in a class the students usually face risk and the teacher can relax).

The performance of STUCK, I am claiming, is a social occasion. The sign STUCK symbolized the semantic structure of a conceptual unit that is used in formulating what is happening in the deaf education classrooms at Northfield. Along what cultural dimension is this social occasion organized? I suggest that its major dimension is power. The struggle for power appears to play an important role in the cultural structure of the deaf education classroom.[7]

This is of course exactly what one would expect if my characterization of deaf education, after Freire, as a pedagogy of the oppressed, holds true. The teachers control the power, and the deaf students are essentially powerless. STUCK shows that deaf students are sensitive to this situation. Using the sign

---

[7]This is not unique to this situation; the dimension of power plays an important role in many cross-cultural encounters (Brislin 1981).

is an act of rebellion against the situation. STUCK seeks to re-place power in the hands of the deaf students. In a sense, STUCK is saying, 'I've got power over you; I am able to put you in your place.' It takes the aggression directed at the deaf stu-dent (the aggression of unaccepting) and redirects it at the teacher. This is accomplished not only semantically but also in vivid physical action. The body posture and the "pounding" sound that accompany STUCK are iconic cues that violence is being acted out here. The addressees of STUCK were, remem-ber, female hearing teachers; STUCK was created by and used mostly by boys. STUCK was a threatening and frightening sign.

I have described the semantic extension of a single lexical item in American Sign Language. This sign, STUCK, enacted the production of a particular social scene in the situation of one deaf education program. The scene was short lived. It was cre-ated, had its heyday, and began to disappear all within the period of less than two years. I have also related this scene to the notion of differing cultures. Does this mean than an aspect of Deaf culture at Northfield is also disappearing? On the con-trary. Culture is not the scene itself. Rather culture is the "set of principles for creating dramas, for writing scripts, and, of course, for recruiting players and audiences" (Frake 1980b). This one scene had a relatively short run. Some of the players have left the scene. But school culture, the joint accomplishment of hearing and deaf people in America (and likewise the result of their struggles), ensures that similar scenes will be staged. For one hundred and fifty years of deaf education in America the scenes have been but variations on the same theme. Until we, hearing and deaf people together, change this theme, the closing line will continue to be, "The show must go on."

16

How You Gonna Get to Heaven If You Can't Talk with Jesus?: The Educational Establishment vs. the Deaf Community

James Woodward

THE U.S. Deaf Community offers us unique insights into the nature of how a minority group can maintain linguistic and cultural identity and integrity despite heavy majority oppression. The Deaf community has had to face many of the same linguistic and cultural pressures that various other minority groups in the U.S. have had to face: being viewed as inferior by the majority culture, schooling in an institutional setting, almost exclusive instruction under majority group teachers, discrimination in an exclusion from teacher training programs, forced instruction in the majority language, the prohibition of the minority language in the school, etc. However, the Deaf

Reproduced by permission of the author.

community has had three additional pressures which other groups have not had. (1) The Deaf community has had a more difficult time overcoming inferiority stereotyping by the majority culture than other minority groups, since Deaf people are viewed as a *medical* pathology. (2) In the Deaf community less than 10% of Deaf children have Deaf parents. Thus the majority of Deaf children belong to a different cultural group from their parents and must be enculturated into the minority group through means other than their parents. (3) The primary language of the Deaf community differs not only in code structure but in channel structure from the majority language. Because of this, language oppression has often been doubly sever for Deaf people.

Contrary to the Hearing ethnocentric view of Deaf people as isolated pathological individuals, Deaf people form a thriving community that is held together by such factors as self-identification as a Deaf community member (Padden and Markowicz 1976, Markowicz and Woodward 1975), language (Croneberg 1965, Meadow 1972, Woodward and Markowicz 1975), endogamous marital patterns, and numerous national., regional, and local organizations and social structures (Meadow 1972). Not all hearing impaired individuals belong to the Deaf community, in fact, audiometric deafness, the actual degree of hearing loss, often has very little to do with where a person relates in the Deaf community (Padden and Markowicz 1976).

Attitudinal Deafness (self identification as a member of the Deaf community and identification by other members as a member) appears to be the most basic factor determining membership in the Deaf community (Padden and Markowicz 1976, Markowicz and Woodward 1975). Attitudinal Deafness explains why some hard of hearing persons consider themselves Deaf, why some profoundly hearing impaired individuals claim to be hard of hearing or actually Hearing, and why some young hearing children of Deaf parents may refuse to speak for some time, even though they are quite capable of speaking.

Attitudinal Deafness also helps explain the high incidence of endogamous marital patterns among Deaf people. Fay (1898) records an 85% rate of endogamous marriage and Rainer and others (1963) in a survey of New York found that 95% of marriages of women born deaf and 91% of marriages of women who became deaf at an early age were endogamous. Remembering that the rate of postlingual deafness was much higher in the past due to disease, one can hypothesize that marital patterns have changed very little since the turn of the century and probably before that in the U.S. Deaf community. Also as Woodward and Markowicz (1975) point out, since not all women in the study by Rainer and others were necessarily members of the Deaf Community, the percentages of marriages across the Deaf ethnic boundary is possibly reduced even further.

Attitudinal Deafness is always paralleled by appropriate language use. The language situation in the Deaf community can best be described as a bilingual-diglossic continuum between American Sign Language (ASL) and English (Stokoe 1970, Woodward 1973a). Intermediate varieties along this continuum have been shown to exhibit pidgin-like characteristics (Woodward 1973b, Woodward and Markowicz 1975). Variation along the ASL-to-English continuum is non-discrete, regular, rule-governed, and correlated with a hierarchy of gross social variables. For example, people who consider themselves Deaf, people who have Deaf parents, and people who learned signs before the age of six use language varieties that more closely approach "pure" ASL, while people who are Hearing, people who have Hearing parents, and people who learned signs after the age of six tend to use language varieties less like "pure" ASL. (Woodward 1973a).

Signing that approaches English along the continuum serves as H in the diglossic situation and tends to be used in formal conversations, such as s in church, the classroom, lectures, and with Hearing people. Signing that approaches ASL tends to be used in smaller, less formal, more intimate conversations. Publicly, English is often considered superior to ASL, and ASL is often regarded as ungrammatical or non-existent. Signers generally feel that "grammatical" English should be used instead of ASL for teaching. Much formal grammatical description has been done on English (in its spoken or written form), but only relatively recently has any research on ASL been done. Some signers feel that standardization is necessary, but sign language diglossia appears as stable as other diglossic situations. Deaf children generally learn ASL in the initial locus of enculturation into the Deaf community, normally the family for Deaf children of Deaf parents and the residential school for Deaf children of Hearing parents. Thus sign language diglossia in the U.S. shares the same sociolinguistic characteristics of other languages in diglossic situations (cf. Ferguson 1959, Fishman 1967).

However, no matter what amount of research in the Deaf community and comparative research in other communities can be presented at this time to demonstrate that Deaf people form a minority group with language varieties quite different from English, the Hearing-controlled educational establishment generally still rejects the idea of a Deaf minority group. If the Hearing educational establishment were to recognize the Deaf community as a legitimate minority group, they would soon be forced to admit they know nothing about the structure of the group and that Deaf people could probably help themselves a lot better than Hearing people can.

Such an admission, however, would be counter to the authoritarianism that Vernon, a psychologist, finds so prevalent in Deaf education. Vernon (1972; 15) states: "A deaf child or adult often symbolizes to the authoritarian the very weaknesses and defects he fears himself. Sign language makes the deafness visible whereas its repression 'hides' the defect... Obviously repressing sign language is the first step in the denial of the weakness which deafness symbolizes to the authoritarian. The repression is inevitably rationalized and intellectualized as it remains an unconscious or preconscious motive..." This authoritarianism has existed since the founding of deaf education and has often been manifested in self-proclaimed religious missionary zeal to save Deaf people, hence the title of this paper. Cochrane (1873) in an old discussion of how he viewed the way Deaf students influenced Hearing teachers sums up the religious ethnocentrism and authoritarianism quite well. From my personal experiences, similar attitudes all too prevalently appear in present-day teachers, although they are generally expressed with somewhat more restraint.

Cochrane feels that teaching Deaf students "does not build up the mind; nay, rather it has a tendency to pull down, to lower the standard of previously acquired literary attainments." (Cochrane 1873; 43). Nevertheless, "we are called to labor among those who have no concept of a God; who know nothing of the kind, loving, merciful Father of the universe; whose ears have been closed to the simplest facts of Bible history; whose minds are shrouded in ignorance as dark as that which has settled down upon any of the nations of the earth." (Cochrane 1873; 47). "The teacher's work is to lift the veil that shuts out the beauties and glories of heavenly Jerusalem...so that in time the pupil comes to understand the plan and need of redemption." (Cochrane 1873; 46). Not one to mince words, Cochrane at one point puts his case quite clearly by comparing his contacts with Deaf students to that of his colleagues involved in teaching Hearing children in public schools. "It is very different with the teachers in the public schools, academies, and higher institutions of learning. They are brought in contact with a higher order of intellect." (Cochrane 1873; 44).

These kinds of attitudes of Hearing superiority and Deaf inferiority have led to discrimination in the hiring of Deaf teachers (Moores 1972), especially for young Deaf children, since in almost all schools, whether manually or orally oriented, early education for Deaf children has often stressed speech at the expense of other subjects.

This discrimination has effectively cut off classroom models of Deaf adults for most students until high school age. Some students in residential schools have been lucky enough to have Deaf house parents in the dormitories. This helps, but such obvious job (and pay) discrimination does little to enhance self-concept of Deaf adults or children.

While such discrimination has occurred in other minority groups, it seems that discrimination against Deaf people resulting in language oppression is especially severe and probably

will be harder to overcome because Hearing ideology and technology have labelled Deaf people as abnormal and pathological
characterization is often merely transferred from the individual
to the group (cf. Markowicz and Woodward 1975).

The problem of discrimination in the policy of hiring minority teachers and the resultant language oppression is com-
pounded by the family situation in the Deaf community.

As mentioned earlier, less than 10% of Deaf children have
Deaf parents and are enculturated into the Deaf community in
the home. The other more than 90% of Deaf children have
Hearing parents and are normally enculturated into the Deaf
community in residential schools (Meadow 1972) or, more
rarely, acculturated upon graduation from a Hearing high
school (Lunde 1960, Meadow 1972), or upon entrance into
Gallaudet College (Padden and Markowicz 1976). The majority
of Deaf children of Hearing parents are enculturated into the
Deaf community and its language through peer group Deaf
children of Deaf parents or through slightly older Deaf children
who have already been enculturated into the Deaf community.
Thus most Deaf children have not received meaningful Deaf
cultural input from teachers or family, since teachers and families are mostly Hearing. Authoritarian language oppression can
very easily occur under these situations. As we have already
seen, the schools have tended to repress sign language, especially ASL, and input from deaf adults; and, as we shall see,
even those that permit sign language, discriminate against ASL,
the language varieties that Deaf people normally identify with
(Padden and Markowicz 1976, Markowicz and Woodward
1975). Other minority group children often have a refuge in the
home from such cultural and linguistic oppression. However,
as we have seen, more than 90% of Deaf children who attended
residential schools do not have parents who belong to the same
minority group as they do. Thus Deaf children are much less
protected from cultural and linguistic discrimination than
children from other minority groups.

Now, let us look at some basic characteristics of this
language oppression.

The major issue in language policy for Deaf education has been the oral–manual controversy. Unfortunately, the whole argument, which was started and continued by Hearing people (L'Epee and Heinicke) is based on the peripheral issue of channel (Woodward 1973c). (See Garnett (1968) for some of the earliest statements of this controversy.) Oralism has been advocated strongly since the1880 International Conference of Teachers of the Deaf met in Milan and declared: "The Congress, considering the incontestable superiority of speech over signing in *restoring the deaf mute to society, and in giving him a more perfect knowledge of language,* declares that the oral method ought to be preferred to that of signs for the education of the deaf and dumb" (italics added). Needless to say, almost all delegates to the Conference were Hearing.

This statement, which has heavily influenced language policy in many schools for the Deaf, presumes that there is only one society and one language—the society of Hearing people and the oral language(s) that they use. That there are Deaf communities with their own languages was (and still is to many Hearing educators) and inconceivable violation of ethnocentric beliefs.

It should be pointed out that even the advocates of manualism are generally not purely manual but advocate a combined method of speech and signs that parallel English word order. This variety of signs may vary from the natural pidgin, Pidgin Sign English, that developed out of contact between ASL and English (Woodward 1973b, Woodward and Markowicz 1975) to the artificial sign systems designed to represent English (Bornstein 1973). While it was not necessarily openly stated in all manualist philosophy that signs should parallel English, it is next to impossible to speak English and sign ASL at the same time. One might just as well attempt speaking English and writing French at the same time.

Thus, until recently, there has never been any question that the language code in the classroom should approach English; the question has been through what channel could English be best represented and understood.

With such discrimination against Deaf people and their language in educational policy and with the majority of parents of Deaf children being Hearing, how has the Deaf community been able to maintain its own language? There seem to be three possible reasons for this.

One reason seems to be that the oppression which has confronted the Deaf community has greatly strengthened the ethnic bond that unite people who choose to identify with the Deaf community. Because most Deaf children have not normally had a refuge in the home from cultural oppression, they appear at a very young age to have formed very strong ethnic ties with their peer group to cope with outside threats against self-concept and identity. Some support for this idea comes from Vernon (1972; 13) who states that "prominent existing theories of schizophrenia would assume that the isolation resulting from congenital deafness would seriously enough impair affective functioning and object relations actually to cause schizophrenia. Deafness reproduces many of the key early experiences thought to be primary to this psychosis." However, comparatively speaking, Deaf people are as well adjusted as Hearing people. Early ethnic affiliation may be one of the chief strategies for coping with an essentially hostile environment that is not often overcome with much help from parents.

Deaf consultants have reported to me that they feel that they and other Deaf people who strongly identify with the Deaf community, if forced to interact with an unknown outsider, would rather communicate with a foreign Deaf person than with a Hearing American. This ethnosemantic classification of closer-to-more-distant outsiders helps support the idea of the great strength of ethnic identification with the Deaf community. The second possible reason for the thriving of ASL relates to the channel and code structure of ASL as compared with English. Because Deaf people have hearing impairments, they prefer to use languages channeled through a visual–manual modality rather than through and oral–aural modality. As Hymes (1964,1968) has suggested and as research studies in American Sign Language (Bellugi and Fischer 1972) have shown, language codes are highly constrained by channel. Sign languages are not particularly dependent on linearity and concatenations of inflectional affixes as oral languages tend to be. Instead, sign inflections are most often represented on the surface through internal modifications of the sign. An example of this is Agent–Beneficiary directionality (Woodward 1975) in which the relationship between actor and receiver is represented by movement in three dimensional space by the verb sign, not by linear order of occurrence or by sequential affixing. Sign language phonologies also have a completely different phonetic base physiologically from oral language phonologies. Thus it is impossible to directly transmit oral language phonology in a sign language and vice-versa (Woodward and Markowicz 1975). It seems then that the visual–manual channel of ASL prohibits very great influence from English structure, which is constrained by a different channel.

Thirdly, the diglossic situation in the Deaf community serves as a way of maintaining linguistic and cultural integrity. ASL is preserved since ASL and Pidgin Sign English have completely separate social functions. ASL is used for intimate interaction among members of the Deaf community. Pidgin Sign English is used in classroom situations and in conversations with Hearing people. With these separate functions, there is less likelihood of encroachments from English and a greater possibility of linguistic autonomy within the community. Also because the diglossic situation ensures that Deaf people switch to signing that approaches English around a Hearing person, most Hearing people are effectively barred from learning ASL and thus from actively influencing it. Furthermore, because Pidgin Sign English is a pidgin, it allows for satisfaction of basic communicative but not of integrative or expressive communication needs of members of the Deaf community. Thus, Pidgin Sign English "allows the transmission of information in a code native to neither Deaf nor Hearing individuals, but in a channel to which the Deaf person is clearly more attuned. Information useful to the community and its members can be obtained without sacrificing cultural integrity and group solidarity. There is little chance that Hearing people can actively introduce new and contradictory ideology into the community in a language other than ASL" (Markowicz and Woodward 1975:9).

The Deaf community's preservation of linguistic and cultural traditions in the face of strong oppression exemplifies the ability of people to adapt for survival in addition to pressures faced by other minority groups, the Deaf person has been viewed as a medical pathology, has undergone oppression of linguistic channel and code, and has not often had refuge in the home from sociolinguistic discrimination. The equalizing forces that have allowed the Deaf community to maintain minority language in spite of majority pressure are both social and linguistic. The strengthening of the ethnic bond is a social phenomenon, but it is tied to language, since one of the primary criteria for recognition of Deaf community members is the use of American Sign Language. The manual–visual channel preferred by Deaf individuals does not allow for easy transfer of information from a code transmitted in an oral–aural channel, e.g. English. Finally, the diglossic situation and the pidgin-like nature of Pidgin Sign English provide sociolinguistic buffers that permit American Sign Language to flourish with comparatively little outside influence.

17

Who's Itching to Get into Mainstreaming?

Ben Bahan

FOR A year I have had a bothersome itch that keeps teasing my foot. When I scratch it, it won't go away; it only gets worse.

I went to a podiatrist (a foot doctor), who examined me and declared there was nothing wrong with my foot. I was puzzled and decided I had to discover the culprit behind that itch. Recently I found my answer, though I still endure the itch.

I was reading the May issue of Silent News and discovered an article on Integration. Instantly my foot began to itch like hell. Ahh, there it was: I made the connection between my itching foot and mainstreaming. Now every time I confront that issue I will declare: mainstreaming, my foot!

Resentment Towards Mainstreaming

My feelings aren't mine alone. I feel they reflect the overall resentment the deaf community has towards mainstreaming.

The trend in education today is to integrate (another term for "mainstreaming") students with diversified backgrounds, races, and abilities. Deaf students are guinea pigs in a national

Reproduced by permission of the author and *Deaf Community News*.

experiment being conducted in laboratories (read: schools) across the country.

Before someone hands us official results from the mainstreaming experiment, we can safely state why mainstreaming works for some groups of people while it does not work for others.

Go to the Zoo

In one sense everyone is into integration. You'll find evidences of it being imposed on almost every level of life.

Go to the zoo. You'll find most of the modern zoos have animals roaming around free and having their share of integration (my foot: scratch, scratch).

You hop on a tour bus to take a ride around the zoo (with interpreters one hopes, if integration is to take place). As the bus rolls on, the guide explains the philosophy behind this integrated zoo, that the animals roam about freely and are happy.

As you take a ride around the zoo, though, you can't help noticing that in the midst of the integration speech, the animals are hanging out with their own kind: lions with lions, giraffes with giraffes, and so on.

Creating Social "Harmony"

Let's go back to the supposedly highly-intelligent animal, the human being. Humans deserve a round of applause for striving to create an integrated society. We know integration has had its advantage among people of diversified races. It creates, among young people, social "harmony" and the understanding that to be different isn't monstrous.

It should be understood that integration usually involves people of different color, but the issues of integration are more than skin-deep. There exists a variety of cultural and linguistic differences, which creates a different set of problems. Students may be integrated, but they still will choose to hang around with members of their own cultural/linguistic group.

Integrating Abilities

The point is that integrating on the basis of race is very different from integrating on the basis of communication abilities. More specifically, integrating blacks and whites is not the same as integrating hearing and deaf.

We may be able to integrate successfully on a physical level with hearing people. One deaf student might have made it on a hearing high school field hockey team, being a very aggressive player, winning athletic awards.

But that same student is not completely integrated in terms of communication. That student will miss out a lot, in the locker room, in the bus to away games. That student's communication will probably be limited to the coach and a few selected players.

The system will consider the student's involvement in the high school and field hockey team as a successful form of integration. While inside that student, the person's inner well-being is disintegrating. The student's intellectual/social form of integration has not been met.

Mainstreaming's a Mistake

I speak from observation and experience. I was "integrated" in the first few years of my schoolhood (kindergarten through second grade).

I felt I was physically integrate-able until I was transferred to a school for the deaf, where I discovered I could be integrated in many more levels: physical, social, mental, and spiritual. The key to integration is mutuality among peers and, above all, a complete communication environment.

Some people feel we should mainstream students when they reach high school. This is a big mistake. When students get to high school, they reach a period in life where they start to detach themselves from the nest of "home" and begin associating with peers.

In a hearing high school, the deaf teenager will face a lot of hardship to his/her mental, spiritual and social integrity, though the teen may have a few friends and participate, for example, on a field hockey team.

Incompetent Interpreters

Many programs do detect the gap in communicative needs. So they compensate by hiring interpreters. That's great! My heart extends to interpreters because they assist us in tearing down barriers.

I have one major criticism of the programs: they use incompetent interpreters without proper training or insufficient training and without certification. The overall appearance of mainstreaming programs looks good now, with someone moving his/her hands in front of a classroom of integrated students.

Beware of this deceiving look! The interpreter may not be interpreting everything: the deaf students will still miss out on the hearing students' vocal intonations, tones, and moods that are conveyed through the auditory channel.

Incompetent interpreters don't have the training to convey that. All the supposedly-integrated classroom isn't possible, even with interpreters (skilled or unskilled) because so many things are missed.

One reason is the difference in input channels: deaf perceive by eyes, hearing by ears (in terms of language exchanges). This alone requires different pragmatic functions (ways and rules to express and receive information) which will need different paces to keep the integrated students involved in the classroom dynamics.

Why Not Ask Us?

I want to throw in one hypothetical situation and one question. The deaf community on the whole (maybe some individuals, but not the whole community) was not asked its opinion and desire to integrate/mainstream deaf children in hearing schools.

We were just thrown into this situation by legislative acts performed by hearing people. If they sincerely want to integrate us, wouldn't it be sensible for them to ask us as a community if we wanted to be integrated and how we feel about this issue?

If integration is to work, it has to work first outside of the education establishment before we can bring it into the schools. It projects an artificial picture of what the world is really like. Deaf children graduate from school and go out facing the de-segregated society and end up hanging around with other deaf people.

So much for integration.

Ohh, my foot! Scratch, scratch.

18

Breaking Through the Culture of Silence

Sherman Wilcox

We were simply talking in our language of signs,
When stormed by anthem-driven soldiers
pitched a fever by the score of their regime.
They cuffed our hands, strangled us with iron reins.
"Follow me! Line up! Now sit!"
The captain, whip in hand,
inflicts his sentence with this command:
Speak!
"Sh..?"
Speak!
"..i..?"
Speak!
"..t?"
Damn your chains!
We'll pronounce our own deliverance
and articulate our message loud and clear.

And for the width of a breath we grant each other asylum
talking in our language of signs.

When ... they pound, pound, pound.
"Don't answer. Don't open. It's bad, don't!"
The thunder rolls again.

179

"But I want to. I want to see.
Well maybe. I just want to see."
So step by step we succumb
our silent agreement, undone.

"Come out of your dark and silent world
and join us in our bright and lovely world."

Look! Those whose ears work are signing.
Yes, but such queer speech they shape.
What waits out there? To be fair we should see more.
Could it be they've rearranged their score?

And one-by-one
we go down the corridor of their sterile syntax,
not knowing ...

(excerpt from an untitled poem, Ella Lentz)[1]

MY PRESENTATION is unabashedly political. The message I want to leave is this: the Deaf community is an oppressed, disempowered minority. One way that power has been withheld from Deaf students is the systematic confounding of their linguistic situation. As a result the development of literacy is both a problem and a solution.

One of the most crippling problems in deaf education today is the pervasiveness of myths surrounding Deaf people, their language, and their lives. These obscuring myths would be mere trifles if they did not have such a powerful influence on Deaf people; these mythical trivialities can determine the living realities of Deaf students.

Interactionism is the framework I will use to describe the influence of myths on Deaf people's language and learning. It is based on the writing of the Russian psychologist Vygotsky

---

[1]Transcription by the author of a translation of the poem which appeared on the videotape *American Culture: The Deaf Perspective (Literature).*

(1962, 1978) as expanded by Vera John-Steiner and her associates (John-Steiner 1985, Elsasser and John-Steiner 1977, John-Steiner and Tatter 1983). The interactionist framework assumes that: (1) language is both a tool for thinking and a tool for communicating; (2) the use of language as a communicative tool can and should be studied as social interaction; and (3) language develops and is used in social-historical contexts. The strength of the interactionist approach to literacy is that it encourages us to examine how society and its myths and ideologies—our "cultural residue" as Paulo Friere (1985) would say—become internalized by individuals. This internalized residue affects language and the development of literacy. But because language is also a tool for thinking, the critical examination of these myths can become a means to illuminate reality.

An interactionist understanding of literacy in the Deaf community is important for two reasons. First, interactionism readily incorporates the fact that deafness is above all not a pathological problem. Deafness is not a problem that can be "cured" by fixing and filling. Deafness is in essence a cultural problem, one that must be understood in terms of power. The central problems of Deafness and Deaf literacy are locked in the struggle for power; power defined, as Foucault would say, in terms of "who is charged with saying what counts as true knowledge" (1980:131). Second, interactionism stresses that literacy is an effective means of questioning myths. Literacy programs can "challenge the myths of our society" (Holt 1965:8). Literacy is a vehicle for liberation because it promotes critical thinking and empowerment (Giroux 1983).

The radical educator, Henry Giroux, has written that if we are to understand the meaning of liberation we must first be aware of the form that domination takes by examining the historical and cultural particularities of subordinate and oppressed groups. Here I would like to explore a few particularities that shape the consciousness of deaf people: our ideologies surrounding languages perpetuated in our talk about signing, signed languages, and language; our understanding of who Deaf people are; our educational practices. All these in a subtle but powerful way withhold knowledge from deaf people. Deaf people are kept unconscious of their own linguistic situation, and thus they are unable to transform that situation. As Ella puts it in the poem, Deaf people "go down the corridor ... NOT KNOWING."

Deaf children and adults live in a bilingual and trimodal environment. By this I mean that within deaf education and the Deaf community there are three ways of "doing" a language: speaking, writing, and signing; and there are two languages: English (which may be spoken, written or signed) and American Sign Language (which can be signed only).

The first way in which Deaf people are "mythified" is in understanding the relationship between languages and their perceptible expression. Hearing people dealing with deaf people, perhaps unknowingly, switch logical types. It works this way.

Suppose someone were to walk into a lecture room and start speaking some language that you had never heard before. You might lean over to your neighbor and ask, "What *is* that?" Now, imagine that your neighbor discreetly whispers back, "That's speech;" or "That's spoken language." We know immediately that something is wrong here. You asked "What is that?" to know what language is being used, and your neighbor has answered as if you were asking what mode is being used—answered "speech." Languages and the mode of expression of them belong to different logical types: mixing types leads to complete confusion.

Or suppose I were to write some strange characters on the blackboard, you again ask, "What is that?" and your neighbor answers "Written language," or "Writing." Nobody, of course would be so perverse as to answer our questions like this. These answers are not acceptable; we immediately see that they are answers to the wrong question. Yet, it is perfectly acceptable, when asked what a deaf person is doing when she moves her hands to say "Oh, that's sign language."

Our talk (our culturally fixed way of thinking) about signing and signed languages confuses the use of hands, the modality, with a language. Signing is not a language but only a means of producing (utterances of) a language. This is important because in education for the deaf and in the Deaf community there are two languages that are signed—produced with the hands: English and American Sign Language, or ASL.

ASL is a visual-gestural language used in the United States and Canada by Deaf people. It is not universal and it is not English; it has its own phonology, morphology, syntax, and semantics. It can only be signed; you can't speak or write ASL. Literature in ASL is necessarily "oral literature," not preserved in a permanent medium like writing but handed down from one signer to another, one generation to another.[2]

What about signing English? If you could see Ella signing her poem on the video tape, a poem that uses both ASL and English, you would be struck by the difference, the tension visible when she uses signed English. When the teacher in the poem beckons, "Come out of your dark and silent world," Ella code-switches to a kind of signed English that she signs in a very mocking, derogatory style.

Unlike ASL, signed English systems are the inventions of educators. Signed English—or Englishes; there are several systems for encoding English in signs—was designed for the express purpose of making English visible to deaf students. The several systems of signed English differ in how they answer two basic design questions: first, what level of English are we going to represent (sounds, morphemes, words, suprasegmentals, etc.)? and second, where are we going to get our stock of "signs" (by outright invention or by borrowing from the already existing stock of ASL signs)?

Some systems, notably Cued Speech, have approached the design of signing English by using newly created gestures to represent the sounds (phonemes) of English. They are not widely accepted. The more successful systems of signed English have answered these two questions in a conservative manner. They have chosen to represent by manual signs whole words of English, for the most part, with an occasional inflectional or

---

[2]Videotape technology now offers a way to preserve the oral literature of ASL in a permanent record.

derivational morpheme thrown in for convenience—the latter are usually called "sign markers;" and they have borrowed extensively from ASL's stock of lexical items. Thus if one signs READ or WRITE in ASL and in English, it is clear that the same signs are used in both.

These design decisions were made by the creators of signed English systems in order to make their systems more accessible and acceptable to the Deaf community. For example, Harry Bornstein, one of the originators of "Signed English," states that "most of the signs in Signed English are taken from ASL... We use ASL signs where possible because it should make it somewhat easier for the child to communicate with people who use that language" (Bornstein et al. 1983:4). This is a laudable goal. There is another side to the story, though, because this design decision also confuses Deaf students by obscuring the differences between the languages ASL and English. Many words in signed English end up looking the same as ASL words. Bornstein recognizes the need to warn parents of deaf children about this: "American Sign Language is different from English, so do not be surprised if you have difficulty communicating with those deaf adults who depend exclusively on ASL" (ibid.). My question is, who is warning the deaf students with whom teachers use signed English?

One characteristic of weak writers is that they often approach writing as a translation task, from the spoken word to the written word. Deaf children and adults also seem sometimes to approach writing as a translation task—a translation of signed "word" to written word. This is especially a problem for Deaf literacy because of the relationship between signed words and written words, more specifically between ASL words and English words. The relationship is already skewed because of the design of signed English systems. But there is more.

Unlike English, ASL is a polysynthetic language. Words in ASL are very different from words in English. Words in ASL can be verbs that incorporate subjects and objects within themselves, while presenting also complex adverbial, temporal, and other information. Our talk, the talk of those inculturated in hearing cultures, about signed language works to subvert the

Deaf student's understanding of this situation. We commonly teach, with a gestural demonstration, "This is how we sign X," inserting at 'X' an English word. WE who hear also ask deaf teachers of signs questions about how "to sign" English words, and we expect that because we are asking a question about one word of English, the answer, the ASL equivalent, will be one sign also. The relationship between polysynthetic ASL signs and English written words presents problems for the Deaf writer, as in the following note:

> I must know now not postpone postpone postpone...
> Manager and else new manager woman Fern will not
> be no any more her manager fired.

The writer seems to have assumed that the multi-morphemic, trisyllabic inflected ASL verb POSTPONE must be written as three instances of the English word.

It is also important to examine the signed "equivalent" of a word. Is a signed word only what is on the hands, or is it something more? For example, does the signed word include information from the face, body posture, or other sources?

The second question has to do with the nature of ASL words. They do contain information from other sources than just the hands. The assumption that information in ASL is presented only by the hands is a culturally imposed myth, and it raises a serious barrier to linguistic description. From the research of those like Charlotte Baker-Shenk of the discontinued Linguistics Research Laboratory at Gallaudet College and Scott Liddell in the Linguistics Department of Gallaudet University, linguists now know that ASL words are not solely represented by action of the hands. This also can be a problem for Deaf students who approach the task of writing English as a translation of signed words, which in their conception are represented only on the hands, into written words. For example "question-markers" in ASL are complex configurations of facial and head action. This seems to have been a problem for the Deaf writer in this note:

> Sherman—don't forget you bring the picture tomor-
> row. OK.

I am certain that the sign OK would have been signed with an accompanying question-marker (just as one speaks "OK?" with a question inflection). Since our talk about ASL does not recognize that the multi-morphemic ASL words can contain information in locations other than the hands (in this case, on the face), the student neglected to translate the question-marker into her written English.

Many more, and probably more eloquent, examples of this type could be given, but these should make the point; and now the reader may wonder, "what does all this have to do with the culture of silence?"

Freire has said that

> ... in the culture of silence the masses are mute ... They are prohibited from taking part in the transformations of their society and therefore prohibited from being. Even if they can occasionally read and write because they were "taught" in humanitarian—but not humanist—literacy cam-paigns, they are nevertheless alienated from the power re-sponsible for their silence. (1985: 50)

We think of Deaf students as "disabled," but this is true only if we realize that the source of the disablement is not within the students. It is not the pathology of their deafness. Deaf students are *rendered unable* or disabled by their interac-tions and struggles with the more powerful Hearing educa-tional establishment and by the myths that I have described briefly here, myths that are perpetuated in our educational methods, our talk about signing, and our understanding of the Deaf cultural situation. Deaf students, like the minority stu-dents that Cummins describes (1986), are differentially disabled or empowered by their school experience.

Far too often Deaf people are surrounded by a culture of silence—not the silence of not being able to hear or speak but the silence of not being heard, of not having a "voice." Again, in the words of Henry Giroux, " to be voiceless in a society is to be powerless. Literacy skills can be emancipatory only to the degree that they give people the critical tools to awaken and liberate themselves from their often mystified and distorted view of the world" (1983: 228). How then can we break through the culture of silence? How can Deaf people's Deafness become the source of their own empowerment?

One way is to enlighten Deaf students about the true nature of their linguistic situation. This doesn't mean that Deaf students need to become linguists. It does mean that increased metalinguistic awareness can provide distance from a "mystified and distorted view of the world." By objectifying their world, Deaf students can begin to know it and question it in a critical way. We can begin by teaching Deaf students about signed, spoken, and written modes and about the differences between ASL and English (differences often obscured by word-sign), and about the true complexity of the bilingual, trimodal task they face.

We have the testimony of Deaf persons themselves that this way does enlighten. Mervin Garretson in his Foreword to Sign Language and the Deaf Community writes, "To know, once and for all, that our 'primitive' and 'ideographic gestures' are really a formal language on a par with all other languages of the world is a step towards pride and liberation" (Baker and Battison 1980:vi). Barbara Kannapell writes, in the same volume: "Once I learned that ASL is my native language, I developed a strong sense of identity as a deaf person and a more positive self-image" (*op. cit.* 112).

Another way to start chipping away at the culture of silence is by exploring Deaf culture's own "generative themes" in literacy programs. I have seen the beginnings of many "generative themes" when Deaf people tell stories about something that happened to them, in which the moral of the story is that Deaf people must be careful to rely on their eyes. The eyes and vision play a critical and hitherto unexplored role in Deaf culture. To explore this, Deaf students in school may be asked to write on the importance of eyes. Here is an example from an assignment I gave a deaf student in a public high school. He called it, "How to skill eye with the Deaf."

> The paragraph is about ear as not hear with deaf.
> When I was little boy I usually used my eyes for driving
> carefully. I walked across the street and the car honked me. I
> can't hear it. The other story about is bike. My brother teach
> me to how ride bike then I learn to ride it. Then when the car
> arrived near my home it hit almost me. I ride on the street
> the car was horn to me. Please moved side street. The car
> horn many again to me. The woman said Pleas moved by
> side street. I told I am Deaf. The woman said oh I see but you
> need you eye look car. I feel better eye look car. I said no
> problem.

I don't believe any of these activities will alone bring improved literacy skills for Deaf students. The first crack in the Deaf community's culture of silence will not come from outside activity. These activities will, however, result in a more active, more critical consciousness on the part of Deaf students. And this in turn will empower Deaf students, allowing them, in Henry Giroux's words, to "produce, reinvent, and create the ideological and material tools they need to break through the myths and structures that prevent them from transforming an oppressive social reality" (1983:226).

The culture of silence must be broken from within, and the first blow must come from the Deaf student. As Nan Elsasser and Vera John-Steiner have noted: "A student's sense of personal power and control emerges largely as a result of the increasing movement of his or her social group towards self-determination. In the absence of such movement educational intervention is most often futile" (1977:56f). Or, as Ella Lentz so eloquently expresses it: "Damn your chains! We'll pronounce our OWN deliverance and articulate OUR message loud and clear."

19

The War is Not Over

Ben Bahan

"DEAF PRESIDENT Now, Deaf President Now, Deaf President Now!" was the battle cry of the masses that marched to Capitol Hill last March. It was a signed demand the world heard.

In one tumultuous week the students of Gallaudet overthrew a 124 year old institutional structure that was dominated by hearing people. In one week the students told the world, "We are tired of this domination. We want to turn the institution over into our own Hands."

And govern we will!

The whole event is title, in Jack Gannon's (1989) book, *The Week the World Heard Gallaudet*.

My biggest fear is it will end there: *one week*. In reality we have only won one battle. The war is not over—it has not yet begun!

It's time we begin and tell the social institution we are tired of being dominated.

We need to raise consciousness on the state of deaf education. We can start by outlining what should be done. First, let us look at the purpose of the Gallaudet protest: Giving the control of our lives back to us (why did I say back? We never had it in the first place.). Giving the power structure, the administrative jobs, to the Deaf people. In short we want to run

---

Reproduced by permission of the author and *Deaf Community News*.

our educational institutions for, of and by the Deaf. We are the best models, we know it. We know what's best, we have lived it.

We do not have enough Deaf teachers; it is a crisis. We must demand more Deaf teachers. Ideally we should demand that at least 50 percent of the teachers be Deaf. Why settle for less? The Deaf children in schools comprise 100 percent of the student body (including hard of hearing), and the schools have the nerve of only employing a small percentage (nationwide statistics: approximately 10%) of Deaf teachers. Some schools claim to have a high number of Deaf employees, but don't let those numbers fool you. Most of the Deaf employees are not in faculty or teaching positions. Most of them are staff members such as teachers aides and dorm counselors. What about positions in which they have direct control in shaping the minds of Deaf children? The numbers at that power level are dangerously low. We are definitely in crisis!

How many Deaf people have administrative positions? I can think of a very few at that level of power structure. How many Deaf superintendents are there in Massachusetts or New England? NONE!

Remember the battle cry at Capitol Hill in Washington, DC? Deaf President Now! We should seize the momentum and spell out four demands:

1) that 50 percent of the teachers be Deaf
2) that American Sign Language and Deaf culture be an integral part of the curriculum
3) that at least 50 percent of the school board be Deaf; that we be empowered to make decisions regarding the policies implemented by the Department of Education regarding the education of Deaf children
4) and that we have DEAF SUPERINTENDENTS NOW!

We have been discriminated against by the educational and social institutions for too long. We should demand that they start discriminating in our favor, meaning they start looking for and *hiring only Deaf people* for at least 10 years (they should be grateful, because we have been discriminated against since time began). We should require active recruitment of Deaf teachers, starting with admitting more Deaf students to teacher training programs.

Some Deaf people will probably start arguing that, "Well, what if we encounter a really qualified hearing person? Are we expected to turn that person down just because he or she hears?" We'll say yes, because for a long time we have been turned down because we can't hear.

Is the failure ours or theirs? Maybe it is not their fault, for they do not really know what it is like. In one way maybe the whole purpose of deaf education has been to "domesticate" us—like farm animals. To make us believe we are not capable as teachers because our English or speech isn't good enough. We are judged by a language (English) to which we have no access except through artificial means such as oralism, Signing Exact English, and reading and writing. So in the end, we are trained to be underqualified in mastering the language of the dominators. It is little wonder that in their eyes, we are not fit to teach. We have been "domesticated" into settling for meager jobs.

If the power structure produced well-trained Deaf teachers, then we would have been taught by Deaf people who are part of the power structure. That would motivate us to move on, to climb for a better standard of living. In the videotape series, "American Culture: The Deaf Perspective—Deaf Heritage" (produced by the San Francisco Public Library) Jack Gannon, author of *Deaf Heritage*, was asked to single out a Deaf individual who he felt had a big contribution to the heritage of the Deaf people. He replied, "I don't think I can single out one person. I think maybe I would give most of the credits to Deaf teachers, because they started everything. If it wasn't for Deaf teachers who challenged, helped, taught, and inspired Deaf children, I don't think many Deaf people would succeed as well as they did today."

So, as we place our argument on the table, we go back to the notion that we should demand Deaf teachers be hired consistently for 10 years. Along with the other *four demands we place in front of us, we can and will change the educational institution.*

A state school for the deaf in Massachusetts is a great dream, *but an even greater dream still is the day we take power of our own educational and cultual destiny.*

When we strive to do this, in the future Jack Gannon may entitle his forthcoming book: *The Decade the World Heard Gallaudet!* We only won one battle. THE WAR IS NOT OVER!

References

Alterman, A. (1970). Language and the education of children with early profound deafness. *American Annals of the Deaf* 115 , 514–521.

Anthony, A. and associates (Eds.). (1981). *Seeing essential English/manual.* Anaheim, California: Educational Services Division, Anaheim Union School District.

Baker, Charlotte. (1977). Regulators and turn-taking in ASL discourse. In L. Friedman (Ed.), *On the other hand: New perspectives on American Sign Language.* New York: Academic Press.

—. (1980). Sentences in ASL. In Baker, Charlotte and Battison, Robbin, (Eds.), *Sign language and the deaf community: Essays in honor of William C. Stokoe.* (pp. 75–88). Silver Spring, MD: The National Association of the Deaf.

Baker, Charlotte, and Battison, Robbin, (Eds).(1980). *Sign language and the deaf community: Essays in honor of William C. Stokoe.* Silver Spring, MD: The National Association of the Deaf.

Baker, Charlotte & Cokely, D. (1980). *American Sign Language: A teacher's resource text on grammar and culture.* Silver Spring, MD: TJ Publishers, Inc.

Baker, Charlotte & Padden, C. (1978). *ASL: A look at its history, structure, and community.* Silver Spring, MD: TJ Publishers, Inc.

Baratz, J.C. (1969). Teaching reading in an urban negro school system. In Baratz, J.C. and R.W. Shuy (Eds.), *Teaching black children to read* (pp. 92–116). Washington, DC: Center for Applied Linguistics.

Bascom, William R. Four functions of folklore. In Alan Dundes (Ed.), *The study of folklore* (pp. 270–298). Englewood Cliffs, NJ: Prentice-Hall.

Basso, Keith.(1979). *Portraits of "The white man": Linguistic play and cultural symbols among the western Apache.* Cambridge, England: Cambridge University Press.

—. (1976). "Wise words" of the western Apache: Metaphor and semantic theory. In Basso & Selby (Eds.), *Meaning in Anthropology*. Albuquerque, NM: University of New Mexico Press.

Bell, Colin and Newby, H. (1971). *Community studies*. London: George Allen & Unwin, Ltd.

Bellugi, U. and Fischer, S. (1972). A comparison of sign language and spoken language. *Cognition, 1–2/3*, 173–200.

Bellugi, U. And Klima, E. (1972, June). The roots of language in the sign talk of the deaf. *Psychology Today*, pp. 61–64.

Bender, Ruth. (1970). *The conquest of deafness: A history of the long struggle to make possible normal living to those handicapped by lack of normal hearing*. Cleveland: Case Western Reserve University Press.

Bereiter, C. and Engelmann, S. (1966). *Teaching disadvantaged children in the preschool*. Englewood Cliffs, NJ: Prentice-Hall.

Bergson, Henri. (1911). *Laughter: An essay on the meaning of the comic*. (C. Brereton and F. Rothwell, Trans.). New York: McMillan.

Bonvillian, J.D., Charrow, V.R. and Nelson, K.E. (1973). Psycholinguistic and educational implications of deafness. *Human Development, 16,* 321–345.

Bornstein, H. (1973). A description of some current sign systems designed to represent English. *American Annals of the Deaf 18:1,* 41–463.

Bornstein, H., Saulnier, K. and Hamilton, L. (1983). *The comprehensive signed English dictionary*. Washington: Gallaudet College Press.

Bragg, Bernard. (1973). Ameslish: our national heritage. *American Annals of the Deaf, 118,* 672–674.

Brasel, K. and Quigley, S.P. (1975). *The influence of early language and communication environments on the development of language in deaf children*. Champaign-Urbana, Illinois: Institute for Research on Exceptional Children.

Brislin, R.W. (1981). *Cross-cultural encounters: Face-to-face interaction*. NY: Pergamom Press.

Caccamise, Frank, & Hicks, Doin (Eds.). (1980). Proceedings of the second national symposium on sign language research & teaching. Silver Spring, MD: National Association of the Deaf.

Charrow, Veda. (1975). A psycholinguistic analysis of 'deaf English'. *Sign Language Studies* , 7, 139–150.

—. (1975b) Manual English—A linguist's viewpoint. Paper presented at the VIIth World Congress of the World Federation of the Deaf, Washington, DC.

Charrow, V.R. and Fletcher, J.D. (1975). English as the second language of deaf children. *Devel. Psychol.*, 10 (4), 463–470.

Cochrane, M.A. (1873). What influence has teaching the deaf and dumb upon the teacher himself? *American Annals of the Deaf 18* (1), 41–49.

Croneberg, C. (1965). The linguistic community. In William Stokoe, Dorothy Casterline, and Carl Croneberg, *A dictionary of American Sign Language* (pp. 297–312). Washington, DC: Gallaudet College Press.

Cummins, J. (1986). Empowering minority students: A framework for intervention. *Harvard Educational Review, 56,* 18–36.

Douglas, Mary.(1968). The social control of cognition: Some factors in joke perception. *Man 3,* 361–376.

Dundes, Alan.(1973). *Mother wit from the laughing barrel: Readings in the interpretation of Afro-American folklore.* Englewood Cliffs, NJ: Prentice-Hall.

Eastman, Gilbert. (1974). *Sign me Alice: A play in sign language.* Washington, DC: Gallaudet College.

Edwards, Allan and Jones, D. (1976). *Community and Community Development.* The Hague, Netherlands: Mouton & Co.

Elsasser, N. & John-Steiner, V. (1977). An interactionist approach to advancing literacy. *Harvard Educational Review, 47,* 355–369.

Erickson, Frederick, & Shultz, J. (1982). *The counselor as gatekeeper: Social interaction in interviews.* NY: Academic Press.

Erting, Carol. (1978). Language policy and deaf ethnicity in the United States. *Sign Language Studies, 19,* 139–152.

Fant, Louie J., Jr. *Ameslan.* (1972). Northridge, CA: Joyce Motion Picture Co.

—. (1972). *Some preliminary observations on the grammar of Ameslan (American Sign Language).* Unpublished paper. California School for the Deaf, Berkeley.

Fay, E.A. (1898). *Marriages of the deaf in America.* Washington, DC: Volta Bureau.

Feinberg, Leonard. (1978). The secret of humor. *Maledicta, 2,* 86–110.

Ferguson, Charles. (1959). Diglossia. *Word, 15,* 325–340.

Fischer, S. and Gough, B. (1979). Verbs in American Sign Language. In U. Bellugi and E. S. Klima (Eds.). *The Signs of Language.* Cambridge, Mass.: Harvard University Press.

Fishman, J. (1967). Bilingualism with and without diglossia: Diglossia with and without bilingualism. *Journal of Social Issues, 23(2),* 29–38.

Foucault, M. (1980). *Power/Knowledge.* New York: Pantheon Books.

Frake, Charles O. (1980a). The ethnographic study of cognitive systems. In C. O. Frake (Ed.), *Language and Cultural Description.* Stanford, CA: Stanford University Press.

—. (1980b). Plying frames can be dangerous: Some reflections on methodology in cognitive anthropology. In above.

Freire, Paulo. (1970). *Pedagogy of the oppressed.* NY: Seabury.

—. (1985). *The politics of education: Culture, power & liberation.* South Hadley, MA: Bergin & Garvey.

Fry, William. (1963). *Sweet madness: A study of humor.* Palo Alto, CA: Pacific Books.

Furth, H.G. (1971). Linguistic deficiency and thinking: Research with deaf subjects 1964–1969. *Psychol. Bull., 74,* 58–72.

Furth, H.G. and Youniss, J. (1971). A comparison of deaf and hearing subjects. *Int. J. Psychol., 6,* 49–64.

Gallaudet, E.M. (1873). "Deaf-mute" conventions, associations, and newspapers. *American Annals of the Deaf 18(2),* 200–206.

Gannon, Jack. (1980). *Deaf heritage*. Silver Spring, MD: The National Association of the Deaf.

Gannon, Jack. (1989). *The week the world heard Gallaudet*. Washington, DC: Gallaudet University Press.

Garnett, C. (1968). *The exchange of letters between Samuel Heinicke and Abbe Charles Michel De L'Epee*. New York: Vantage Press.

Giroux, H. (1983). *Theory and resistance in education: A pedagogy for the opposition*. South Hadley, MA: Bergin & Garvey.

Gordon, Joseph C. (1892). *Notes and observations upon the education of the deaf*. Washington, DC: The Volta Bureau.

Gould, Stephen J. (1982). The importance of trifles. *Natural History* , *91* (4), 16–21.

Gumperz, John J. (1982a). *Discourse strategies*. NY: Cambridge University Press.

—. (1982b). *Language and social identity*. NY: Cambridge University Press.

Gustason, G., Pfeitzing, D., Zawolkow, E., and Norris, C. (1972). *Signing exact English*. California: Modern Signs Press.

Herskovits, Melville J. (1948). *Man and his works: The science of cultural anthropology*. New York: Knopf.

Hillery, George. (1974). *Communal organizations*. Chicago: Chicago University Press.

Holt, L. (Ed.). (1969). The summer that didn't end. New York: Macmillan.

Hymes, Dell. (1964). Towards ethnographies of communication. In Gumperz and Humes (Eds.), The ethnography of communication. *American Anthropologist* 66(6), Part 2, 1–34.

—. (1968). The ethnogrophy of speaking. In Fishman, Joshua (Ed.), *Readings in the Sociology of Language* (pp. 99–138) Mouton: The Hague.

Jacobs, Leo. (1969). *A deaf adult speaks out*. Washington, DC: Gallaudet College Press.

John-Steiner, V. (1985). The road to competence in an alien land: A Vygotskian perspective on bilingualism. In J. Wertsch (Ed.), *Culture, Communication and Cognition*. New York: Cambridge University Press.

—. & Tatter, P. (1983). An interactionist model of language acquisition. In B. Bain (Ed.), *Sociogenesis of Language and Human Conduct*. New York: Plenum Press.

Kannapell, Barbara. (1974). Bilingual education: A new direction in the education of the deaf. *The Deaf American, 26* (10), 9–15.

—. (1980). Personal awareness & advocacy in the deaf community. In C. Baker & R. Battison (Eds.), *Sign Language and the Deaf Community: Essays in Honor of William C. Stokoe*. Silver Spring, MD: National Association of the Deaf.

Klima, Edward, and Bellugi, Ursula. (1979).*The signs of language*. Cambridge, MA: Harvard University Press.

Koestler, Arthur. (1964). *The act of creation: A study of the conscious and unconscious in science and art*. New York: Dell.

Lane, Harlan. (1977). Notes for a psycho-history of American Sign Language. *Deaf American, 29, 3–7*.

Langacker, Ronald W. (1983). *Foundations of cognitive grammar*. Bloomington, IN: Indiana University Press.

Lunde, Anders S. (1960). The sociology of the deaf. In W. C. Stokoe, William (Ed.), *Sign language structure: An outline of visual communication systems of the American deaf*. University of Buffalo. (Occasional Paper 8, of the Studies in Linguistics series.).

Madsen, Willard J. (1982). *Intermediate conversational sign language*. Washington: Gallaudet College Press.

Markowicz, Harry and Woodward, James. (1975, March 13–15). *Language and the maintenance of ethnic boundaries in the deaf community*. Paper presented at the Conference on Culture and Communication held at Temple University.

Marshall, W.J.A. and Quigley, S.P. (1970). *Quantitative and qualitative analysis of syntactic structure in the written language of hearing impaired students*. Champaign-Urbana, Illinois: Institute for Research on Exceptional Children.

Martineau, William H. (1972). A model of the social functions of humor. In Goldstein, Jeffrey H. and McGhee, Paul E. (Eds.), *The Psychology of Humor*. (pp. 101–125). New York: Academic Press.

McCall, E. A. (1965).A generative grammar of sign. Unpublished master's thesis, University of Iowa.

McDermott, R.P. (1982, March). Stages in the ethnography of school failure 1960–1980: From the rhetoric of schooling. Paper presented at the Third Annual Ethnography in Education Research Forum, University of Pennsylvania, Philadelphia.

Meadow, Katharine P. (1972). Sociolinguistics, sign language, and the deaf subculture. In T. J. O'Rourke (Ed.) *Psycholinguistics and total communication:The state of the art.* (pp. 19–33). Washington DC: American Annals of the Deaf.

—. (1975, July–August).The deaf subculture. *Hearing and Speech Action.*

—. (1980). *Deafness and child development.* Berkeley: University of California Press.

Miles, D. (1976).*Gestures: Poetry in sign language.* Northridge, CA: Joyce Publishers, Inc.

Mindel, E.D. and M. Vernon. (1971). *They grow in silence.* Silver Spring, Maryland: National Association of the Deaf.

Moores, D. (1970). Psycholinguistics and deafness. *American Annals of the Deaf, 115,* 37–48.

—. (1972). Communication: Some unanswered questions and some unquestioned "answers". In O'Rourke, T.J. (Ed.). *Psycholinguistics and total communication: The state of the art.* (pp. 1–10).Washington, DC: The American Annals of the Deaf.

O'Rourke, T., Medina, T., Thames, A. and Sullivan, D. (1975, April 15). National Association of the Deaf communicative program skills. *Programs for the Handicapped,* pp. 27–30.

Osgood, Charles. 1971. Explorations in semantic space: A personal diary. *Journal of Social Issues, 27* (4), 5–64.

Padden, Carol and Markowitz, H. (1976). Cultural conflicts between hearing and deaf communities. In *Proceedings of the Seventh World Congress of the World Federation of the Deaf.* Silver Spring, MD: National Association of the Deaf.

—. (1975) *Crossing cultural group boundaries into the deaf community.* Paper presented at the Conference on Culture and Communication, Temple University, Philadelphia.

Paget, G. and Gorman, P. (1969). *A systematic sign language.* London: National Institute for the Deaf.

Poplin, Dennis. (1972). *Communities: A survey of theories and methods of research.* New York: Macmillan.

Quigley, S.P., Smith, N.L., and Wilbur, R. (1974). Comprehension of relativized structures by deaf students. *Journal of Speech and Hearing Research, 17* (3), 325–341.

Rainer, J., Altschuler, K., and Kallman, F. (Eds.). (1963). *Family and mental health problems in a deaf population.* New York: Department of Genetics, New York State Psychiatric Institute, Columbia University.

Schein, Jerome. (1968). *The deaf community.* Washington, DC: Gallaudet College Press.

Schein, Jerome and Delk, Marcus. (1974). *The deaf population in the United States.* Silver Spring, MD: The National Association of the Deaf.

Scollon, R., & Scollon, S.B.K. (1981). *Narrative, literacy, and face in interethnic communication.* Norwood, NJ: Ablex.

Scouten, E. L. (1967). The rochester method, and oral multisensory approach for instructing prelingual deaf children. *American Annals of the Deaf, 112,* 50–55.

Sternberg, Martin L.A. (1981). American Sign Language: A comprehensive dictionary. NY: Harper & Row.

Stokoe, W.C., Jr. (1960). Sign language structures: An outline of the visual communication systems of the American deaf. *Studies in Linguistics,* Occasional Papers 8.

—. (1970). Sign language diglossia. *Studies in Linguistics, 21,* 27–41.

—. (1971). *The study of sign language.* Silver Spring, MD: National Association of the Deaf.

Stokoe, William C., Croneberg, C. and Casterline, D. (1965). *Dictionary of American Sign Language.* Washington, DC: Gallaudet College Press; (1976, Second edition, Silver Spring, MD: Linstok Press).

Switzer, Mary, and Williams, B. (1967, August). Life problems of deaf people. *Archives of Environmental Health, 15* .

Vernon M. (1972). Nonlinguistic aspects of sign language, human feelings and thought process. In O'Rourke, T.J. (Ed.). *Psycholinguistics and Total Communication: The State of the Art* (pp. 11–18). Washington, DC: The American Annals of the Deaf.

Vernon, M. and Koh, S.D. (1970). Early manual communication and deaf children's achievement. *American Annals of the Deaf, 115,* 527–536.

Vygotsky, L. (1962). *Thought and language.* Cambridge, MA: MIT Press.

—. (1978). *Mind in society.* Cambridge, MA: MIT Press.

Wampler, D. (1971). *Linguistics of visual English: An introduction* (booklets). Santa Rosa, California.

Washington State School for the Deaf. (1972). *An introduction to manual English.* Vancouver, WA: The Washington State School for the Deaf.

Wescott, Roger W. (1971). Linguistic iconism, *Language, 47,* (2), 416–428.

Wilbur, R. B. (1976). The linguistics of manual languages and manual systems. In L.L. Loyd (Ed.), *Communication assessment and intervention strategies.* Baltimore, Md.: University Park Press.

Wilbur, R.B. and Jones, M.L. (1974). Some aspects of the acquisition of sign language and English by three hearing children of deaf parents. In LaGaly, M.L., Fox, R.A. and Bruck, S. (Eds.), *Papers from the Tenth Regional Meeting, Chicago Linguistic Society.* Chicago, IL: Chicago Linguistic Society.

Wilbur, R.B. and Quigley, S.P. (1975). Syntactic structures in the written language of deaf students. *The Volta Review, 77* (3), 194–203.

Wilbur, R.B., Quigley, S.P., and Montanelli, D.S. (1975). Conjoined structures in the language of deaf students. *JSHR, 18* (2), 319–335.

Woods, W.H. (1973). *The forgotten people.* St. Petersburg, FL: Dixie Press.

Woodward, James. (1972). Implications for sociolinguistic research among the deaf. *Sign Language Studies 1,* 1–7.

—. (1973). Some observations on sociolinguistic variation and American Sign Language. *Kansas Journal of Sociology*, *9*, 191–200.

—. (1973a). Implicational lects on the deaf diglossic continuum. Unpublished doctoral dissertation in sociolinguistic. Georgetown University.

—. (1973b). Some characteristics of pidgin sign English. *Sign Language Studies*, *3*, 39–46.

—. (1973c). Deaf awareness. *Sign Language Studies 3*, 57–59.

—. (1975). Variation in American Sign Language syntax: Agent-beneficiary directionality. In Fasold, Ralph and Shuy, Roger (Eds.), *Analyzing Variation in Language*. (pp. 303–311). Washington, DC Georgetown University Press.

—. (1980). Sociolinguistic research on ASL: An historical perspective. In C. Baker and R. Battison (Eds.). *Sign language and the deaf community: Essays in honor of William C. Stokoe.* (pp. 117–134). Silver Spring, MD: The National Association of the Deaf.

Woodward, J. and Markowitz, H. (1975, January). *Some handy new ideas on pidgins and creoles: Pidgin sign languages*. A paper presented at the 1975 International Conference on Pidgin and Creole Language, Honolulu. (1980). In W.C. Stokoe (Ed.), *Sign and culture*. Silver Spring, MD: Linstok Press.

Wright, David. (1969). *Deafness*. New York: Stein & Day.

Youniss, J., Furth, H.G., and Ross, B.M. (1971). Logical symbol use in deaf and hearing adolescents. *Develop. Psychol., 5*, 511–517.

NOTES

NOTES

NOTES

NOTES

NOTES

NOTES

NOTES

NOTES

NOTES

NOTES

NOTES

NOTES

NOTES

NOTES